HOW NORMAL PEOPLE GET RICH

AVOID THE TRAPS. BUILD THE WEALTH.

JOSH WEAVER

First edition
Paperback ISBN: 979-8-234-00945-6
Hardcover ISBN: 979-8-234-00944-9

Library of Congress Control Number: 2026904811

Published by Weaver Publishing
Lakewood Ranch, FL

TABLE OF CONTENTS

WHY YOU FEEL BEHIND WHEN YOU WORK HARD

Every worker knew the process.

When equipment jammed, you shut it down, locked it out, and used the tool designed to clear the blockage. The steps were posted at the station and drilled in training.

On one shift, production was behind. An assembly worker saw a jam and skipped the steps. He reached in with his bare hand while the machine was still live. It cycled once and caught his finger.

In the claim file, the injury showed up as a single line:

"Finger amputated in moving equipment."

When you read the notes around it, the pattern is always the same:

"I didn't want to wait."

"It seemed easier."

"I didn't think anything would happen."

If you feel behind right now, you're not imagining it. Costs have risen faster than pay, and the margin for error is thinner than it used to be. Some people are genuinely constrained by income and fixed expenses. Others are constrained by expectations their income can't support. This book doesn't pretend the system is easy or fair. It also doesn't pretend it's closed. If anything within your control can improve your outcome, it starts with doing the steps in the right order.

There is a path to wealth for normal people, and it's built the same way all reliable systems are, step by step.

MY WAKE-UP CALL

I remember logging into my bank account late one night after work. My balance was barely a few thousand dollars. I was only a few years out of college, and I wasn't making great money, but I still felt behind.

I wasn't out of control; I was just winging it. Money came in, bills went out, and whatever was left disappeared without me noticing.

Around the same time, I was in a car accident that forced everything to stop for a moment. Nothing serious, but enough that I was sweating the deductible payment. One unexpected event was all it took to knock my month off course.

I started paying attention to the people around me. Some were moving ahead. Some were stuck in the same loop I was. Their decisions put them in different places.

WHY THIS BOOK HELPS

I've spent my career in risk management watching what happens when small gaps go unaddressed. The damage doesn't come from one big mistake. It builds up slowly, then one trigger sets it off.

According to LendingClub, nearly 60% of Americans live paycheck to paycheck, even with steady jobs. When money plans assume perfect timing and steady progress, they fall apart the moment life interrupts them. Missed paychecks, HVAC repairs, or an ER visit are enough to knock things off course when there's no margin. This book doesn't waste pages. It lays out the fundamentals in an order that makes them doable.

In this book, rich doesn't mean private jets. It means being in control and having options. You start with one solid first step that makes the rest possible. Everything else builds from there.

STOP THE BLEEDING

Most people want to skip this step, but when you don't know where your money is going, every plan will break the moment pressure shows up.

It's easy to think things are fine because you always "figure it out." The bills gets paid. The car gets fixed. The card gets swiped and dealt with later. Life keeps moving, so it feels like the system works, yet figuring it out every month isn't progress. It's survival. And survival mode keeps you stuck right where you are. Step 1 is where you stop scrambling and start building margin so normal life stops resetting you back to zero.

You look at what comes in, what goes out, and where the gaps are. For many households, the math doesn't work the way they think it does, and they don't see it clearly until it's too late.

You get enough clarity to make the month work even when the numbers are tight, and you build your first buffer at the same time. You set aside just enough money to keep everyday problems from knocking you backward.

This step is meant to move quickly. The goal is to gain awareness.

Skip this step and nothing else sticks.

CHAPTER 1

HIT THE GROUND RUNNING

I reviewed a claim where a general contractor rushed a renovation job. The plumber was a no-show, the schedule was tight, and the project was already behind. Instead of slowing down, the contractor grabbed a day laborer to install the toilets.

Most of the installs were fine, but on one toilet, the supply line was cross-threaded. The next day, the line failed. Water ran through the ceiling below, soaked drywall, ruined flooring, and pooled behind cabinets. An hour or two was enough to cause roughly $25,000 in damage. That single shortcut turned a routine job into a major disruption.

Money problems start the same way. Everything feels fine until pressure shows up.

This chapter is about gaining awareness. Seeing where you actually stand, without assumptions, so your next moves are intentional instead of reactive.

YOUR FINANCIAL SNAPSHOT

Before you change anything, you need to see what's actually there.

Open your Notes app or grab a pen and paper. We're taking a quick inventory of the big things.

Start with what you own:

- Your bank accounts with their balances
- Any regular investment accounts
- A quick online estimate of your home value
- A quick online estimate of your car's value

Now list what you owe:

- Credit cards with balances
- Your mortgage balance
- Car loans
- Any other debts

Don't include retirement. It doesn't count for today. Don't list furniture, electronics, or anything around your house.

This list is your financial snapshot. Your cash on hand and your debt. Now you know what you're working with.

START PAYING ATTENTION

From this point forward, track everything you spend. Write down every purchase you make this month. Everything from rent to gas to the late-night ice cream. If money leaves your account, it gets written down.

Record each purchase as it happens. Don't rely on memory. You're not fixing anything yet. You're watching. This is how you find the leaks that don't show up in your budget. What you think you spend and what actually leaves your account are usually two different numbers. Tracking closes that gap.

THE $50 CHALLENGE

Today, find $50 in monthly expenses to cut.

Look at what you spend every month and identify what doesn't earn its place. Cancel streaming services you forgot about. Switch a cell phone plan that has crept up. Call your internet provider and ask for a lower rate. It can be one clean cut or a few small ones. The source doesn't matter.

This step is about proving that money in your life can change immediately when you decide it will.

Now lock the change in. Don't redirect the extra $50 somewhere else. Let it sit and create space. In the next chapter, you'll use that space to build your first buffer.

This is where momentum turns into protection.

CHAPTER 2

YOUR FIRST SAFETY NET

Family Video was the last major video rental chain. They survived because they ran with margin. They owned their real estate, kept debt low, and rented out extra space. When the market shifted, they had options their competitors didn't.

Their margin kept them alive for more than 10 years after their competitors were gone. Households break for the same reason companies do. When you have no cushion, a normal problem takes you down. Whether it's one flat tire or one missed shift, you're left with no room to absorb it.

THE MINI-EMERGENCY FUND

So how much margin do you need to stop getting knocked over? Start with $1,000 to $2,500 as your first target. Where you land depends on your situation and how fast you can save.

According to the Federal Reserve, the median unexpected expense runs about $1,200. That's why this range works. It's based on what actually happens.

Keep this in a separate high-yield savings account. Not in checking. Not in a jar at home. A savings account gives you quick access when you need it, but keeps it just far enough away that you won't blow it. Money in checking doesn't stay put.

If you have a stable job, no children, and low bills, $1,000 should be enough. If you have kids, an unstable income, or life tends to punch you harder, aim for $2,500.

This isn't a full emergency fund. That comes later. This is the starter fund, the money that keeps a problem from turning into a financial mess. A dead car battery or a broken appliance doesn't feel like a crisis on its own, but without a buffer, it can derail an entire month.

THE PUSHBACK

Some people will say, "Shouldn't I invest right away? Isn't that smarter?" Not yet.

Investing at this stage won't fix your flat tire tomorrow. If your only money is in the market and your car breaks down, what's your move? Sell and take a loss? Pay taxes or penalties? Swipe a credit card again? That's not a plan.

First you get grounded, then you grow. There's no reliable shortcut around it.

YOUR FIRST REAL MOVE

Knock this out in 90 days or less. You might have to cut or sell something. You might have to say no to dinners out or push off a purchase you wanted. This is temporary. Three months of effort gives you margin that lasts.

If you can't save $1,000 in 90 days, every other step in this book gets harder. This ability to save shows you how ready you are to change. Do you want to keep getting knocked over, or do you want margin?

The first safety net isn't about perfection. It's about moving forward. Emergencies will hit. Margin decides the damage.

Next comes building a margin fast. You can budget and cut, but sometimes the math still doesn't work. The next chapter is about bringing in extra cash quickly so you can stabilize quicker and stop living on the edge.

CHAPTER 3

MAKING ENDS MEET (WHEN THEY DON'T)

Most households fall behind because the cash timing slips. When outflow beats inflow, even slightly, the system stops working. They delay payments. They use credit to fill the gap. They hope things level out on their own, but the pressure only grows.

This chapter closes that risk. When ends don't meet, you need two fast controls. Cut outflow right away. Raise inflow. These moves buy back margin so the month stops sliding and you can regain control before the next hit shows up.

CUTTING COSTS

Start with the easy cuts. Cancel subscriptions you don't use. The small charges add up each month. Cook at home. Sell what's been sitting in your garage or closet.

But cutting only slows the outflow. You still need more coming in.

FAST CASH WORK

You need cash hitting your account this week. That means simple jobs you can start fast with little or no learning curve.

During COVID, I picked up food delivery to bring in extra money. It wasn't glamorous, but the cash added up. People I knew did the same. One saved for a move. It worked because the money was fast and reliable.

Almost 40% of Americans have a side hustle. More than half say that money isn't extra, it's what keeps their bills paid.

According to ZipRecruiter, the average food delivery driver makes between $18 and $25 an hour. Small handyman jobs often pay more. Tutoring starts at around $20 to $30 an hour. You don't need to do this forever. You only need it long enough to build your buffer.

BUY YOURSELF TIME

Extra income gives you something you haven't had yet: margin. If you're in debt and have no savings, you need cash flow. Free it up by pausing retirement contributions for now.

Most experts push saving no matter what, especially if there's a match, but if you don't have margin, your investments are already at risk. The average 401k hardship withdrawal is almost $6,000. People do this because they have no buffer. Once your buffer is in place and debt is under control, we'll turn retirement back on.

REMEMBER THIS

- Cut the easy stuff first.
- Quick income matters more than perfect plans.
- A short sprint can change your situation fast.
- Margin is worth more than any match right now.

STEP 2:

KILL THE LEAKS

Debt is why your progress feels slow. You can do a lot right and still feel stuck when part of every paycheck is already spoken for.

Payments don't adjust when the month is tight. Interest doesn't pause. Any improvement gets absorbed before it can turn into momentum.

In this step, you lay everything out and commit to a payoff. You stay with it until the balances are gone.

It's also where progress accelerates. Every payment removed gives you more control.

You're not here to manage debt. You're here to remove it.

Kill the leaks. Then move forward.

CHAPTER 4

BURNING THE BRIDGE TO DEBT

Most households don't crash into debt. A tight month hits, so a family puts a few bills on a card. The next month brings another expense, and it happens again.

Debt sticks because you get the benefit now and pay for it later. As long as balances exist, part of every raise, bonus, or side hustle disappears into payments first. Most people aren't overspending by thousands. They're losing hundreds each month to obligations they locked in earlier.

The numbers show how fast that pressure builds. According to LendingTree, the average credit card balance for cardholders with unpaid debt in early 2025 was $7,321, up almost 6% in one year. Less than half of cardholders carry a balance, but for those who do, the cost hits hard. Average APR is over 22%, and new offers now top 24%. Many households pay more than $100 a month just to keep their balance from growing. Most of it came from small purchases they don't even remember.

There's a deeper cost too. A Debt.com survey found that 1 in 3 divorced respondents said credit card debt and financial infidelity played a role. Nearly 70% admitted they or their partner had hidden debt. When money is already spoken for, it spills into decisions, relationships, and trust.

And the industry counts on that. *The Nilson Report* found that credit card companies spent more than $4 billion on advertising in 2024. They spend it because borrowing funds their model and because people return to debt when access stays open.

DEBT PAYOFF METHODS

There are two main debt payoff strategies worth knowing: the snowball and the avalanche.

Take three common debts: a $9,000 student loan at 6%, $3,000 in medical debt at 2%, and a $6,000 credit card balance at 22%.

With the snowball, you attack the smallest balance first and pay minimums on everything else. In this example, you'd clear the $3,000 medical bill first, then roll that payment into the $6,000 card, and finally attack the student loan. Small balances clear fast, and that pace keeps you moving.

With the avalanche, you start with the highest interest rate and work your way down. You would start with the $6,000 credit card at 22%, then move to the student loan, and finish with the medical bill. You save more, but the first win usually takes longer.

Here's why I lean toward the snowball. Most people need visible progress to stay consistent. Pace is what keeps you in the fight. A 2016 study in the *Journal of Consumer Research* found that people using the snowball method were more likely to stick with it, even though it wasn't the most efficient on paper.

That doesn't mean you ignore interest. If you have high-cost, short-term debt such as a payday loan, that fire goes to the front of the line. Use the snowball as your base strategy. Pick your order, write it down, and stick with it.

YOUR DEBT PAYOFF PLAN (STEP BY STEP)

Here's the plan.

1. List every debt. Include the lender, balance, minimum payment, and interest rate.
2. Choose your plan. Snowball, avalanche, or hybrid.
3. Pick your first target. This is the debt you will attack with every extra dollar.
4. Set a timeline. Divide the balance by what you can pay each month.

Tape your plan to the wall. Check it weekly. Stay locked in. In this phase, your focus is the advantage.

While you're paying off debt, don't take on any new debt. That part isn't flexible. No "just this once." No upgrades. No new cards.

I've found there's one move most people never try. Call your credit card company and ask for a lower interest rate.

When you call, keep it simple. Say: "Hi, I've been a customer for a while, and I'd like to see if you can lower my interest rate. Other cards are offering me better terms, but I'd like to stay with you if you can help me out."

Ask, pause, and let them respond. Sometimes they will drop your rate on the spot. Sometimes they won't. If they say no, nothing changes. If they say yes, the payoff speeds up. Every point they drop speeds up your payoff.

THE BALANCE TRANSFER TRAP

If interest is burying you and holding you back, a 0% balance transfer can help, but only if you treat it like borrowed time. Most offers give you 12 to 18 months interest-free, but once that clock runs out, the rate hits hard. Miss a payment or break the terms, and interest can apply retroactively.

Here's how to make it work:

- Know the transfer fee (usually 3% to 5%).
- Divide your balance by the number of promo months and commit to that payment.
- Never swipe that card again.

Do it right and it speeds things up.

Example: Sarah, 28, had $5,000 at 23% interest. She moved it to a card with a 15-month promo. She set up autopay for $334 a month and treated it like a bill she could not miss. 15 months later, the debt was gone.

Jason was 34 and stressing about bills. He tried the same thing, but he let payments slide. When the promo ended, he still owed $3,000. The new 27% rate hit, and he was worse off than before.

Sarah treated the promo like a countdown clock. Jason didn't take it seriously. One followed the plan. One didn't.

WHAT ABOUT MY HOUSE OR CAR?

The next questions that come up are: What about my house? What about my car?

If your current housing situation is manageable, keep it simple. The majority of people will get out of debt in 12 to 24 months with focused effort. Stay consistent.

Housing changes disrupt routines, schools, and family life. Unless the current payment is unsustainable, keeping the home stable reduces stress and prevents new problems while you're paying off debt.

That said, if you're single and renting, cutting a few hundred from rent reduces pressure and shortens the payoff window. If you were already planning to move, just make sure your next place supports your new financial plan.

Now, the car.

When it comes to your current vehicle, start with a few direct questions:

- Is it reliable?
- Does it meet your needs?
- Does the payment fit your plan?

Now test it against the numbers:

- If your car payment is more than 9% of your take-home pay, it's too high. At that level, the payment strains your cash flow and slows the payoff.
- If you can't have it paid off within two years while working your plan, it doesn't fit.

If the car you drive today is reliable and can be paid off quickly, keep it. The goal is to free up cash flow, not to force a quick sale.

Here's a simple case. One borrower had $20,000 left on a truck loan, sold it with $12,000 in equity, and used that cash to buy a $12,000 used sedan outright. Between the payment, insurance, and gas savings, he freed up $500 a month. That one move cut his payoff timeline in half.

Reliable used cars exist. A 7- to 10-year-old Toyota Corolla, Honda Civic, or Mazda 3 with decent mileage and proper care will last for years. The average car on the road is over 12 years old. Cars in that age range are typical to own today.

THIS IS A SPRINT, NOT A MARATHON

The goal isn't to live tight forever. It's to get out of debt as fast as possible so you can move on and start building. The pace you choose here sets the finish date.

This is where you redline the intensity. In a car, redlining means pushing the engine into the red zone on the tachometer. You can't run it that way forever. The sprint works the same way. It's temporary, but it gets you out of debt faster than cruising ever will.

This phase shouldn't last more than 24 months. Any longer than that and you risk burnout.

Marcus was a young professional with $12,000 of credit card debt. He picked up Uber shifts, sold his gaming PC, and got a roommate instead of living alone. 10 months later, it was gone. Cutting the last card was the clear signal this phase was over. He closed the gap fast.

But ignoring the problem leads to a very different outcome.

Picture Anita, 67. She still carries a car loan, credit card balances, and a mortgage. From the outside, she looks successful. She had the house, the car, and the steady job, but none of the freedom. Her idea of retirement isn't an option. Every paycheck is still tied up in debt. Her retirement accounts stayed thin because every extra dollar went to keeping up with payments.

Now, the balances are smaller and the window is largely gone. What should be years of freedom is now more years of work.

The push is temporary. The payoff isn't.

NOW YOU MOVE FORWARD

Here's what changes on payday. Your income stops disappearing into payments. That's the first real benefit of debt freedom.

Now you shift to stability. Your next goal is to finish your emergency fund. What you built so far helped stop the early losses. Now you need a safety net that can absorb a real hit.

That means saving at least 3 full months of expenses. Not income. If you are self-employed or your income is unpredictable, you may choose to build a little more. If anything still feels uncertain, the next step locks those numbers down.

This is also where you restart your retirement savings. From here, the work becomes steadier and the benefits show up faster.

You burned the bridge to debt. There's no going back. And that is what keeps you moving forward.

REMEMBER THIS

- Debt ends when you decide it does.
- The sprint is short. Push hard and finish.
- Every payment breaks the cycle that kept you stuck.
- A car loses value. Don't let it take your wealth with it.
- Balance transfers are a tool, not a bailout.
- Write down your payoff plan and check it weekly.
- No new debt.

STEP 3:

LOCK THE SYSTEM

Up to this point, you've been stabilizing damage and removing constraints. That matters, but it still leaves one problem. If the month isn't locked down, it runs you.

Most people don't have a spending problem. They have a control problem. Bills stack in the wrong weeks. Annual expenses arrive without warning. Nothing out of the ordinary happens, but the month still feels tight.

This step puts those controls in place.

You assign every dollar to a category before the month starts. Fixed costs get anchored. Flexible spending gets boundaries. Routine expenses go into sinking funds so they stop ambushing your cash flow. You track what actually happens so nothing hides.

You can't build wealth on a month that won't hold its shape.

CHAPTER 5

SPEND WITHOUT GUILT

When I evaluate the risk of a company with a fleet, it's predictable who will perform well. The best businesses run tight systems. They track how every truck is driven, check driving records every year, and follow their rules the same way every time. Their maintenance plan is documented, and clean inspection data proves it. Their controls stop small issues from growing.

Households work the same way. Spending drifts. Bills sneak up. Stress builds because nothing is planned. A month with no system breaks fast. A budget makes the numbers visible, and visible numbers are harder to ignore.

Zero-based budgeting is the household version of a tracking system. It gives you visibility and stops the drift before it becomes pressure. The household with controls will always perform better than the one that waits for problems to hit.

GETTING STARTED WITH YOUR FIRST BUDGET

The goal is to account for every dollar of your income. By the end of this process, your income minus all your expenses and savings should equal zero. That doesn't mean you're spending everything. It means nothing is left floating around.

Start by listing your income. Use your actual take-home pay, the amount that hits your bank account after taxes and deductions.

If your income varies, use the lowest amount you can count on. For example, a server who averages between $2,200 and $3,000 should budget on the lower number.

Next, list out your fixed expenses. These are the things that stay mostly the same each month: rent or mortgage, insurance premiums, subscriptions, and so on.

Then list your variable expenses such as groceries, gas, eating out, and entertainment. This is anything that shifts from month to month but still happens regularly. You'll see the patterns fast.

After that, subtract your total expenses from your income. If you bring home $4,000 and your expenses total $3,200, that means you have $800 left to assign to savings, extra debt payments, or future goals. Put each dollar in a category so you know where it's going.

Here is a simple example of how it comes together:

- Rent: $1,200
- Groceries: $500

- Car: $350
- Insurance: $150
- Utilities: $200
- Fun Money: $200
- Debt Payments: $600

That totals $3,200. With $4,000 in income, you still have $800 to assign to savings or future goals.

In the beginning, track all your expenses from bills to coffee runs to impulse purchases. The goal is clarity. Once you see it, the rest gets easier.

Give it 3 months. The first month will be rough. The second month gets easier. By month three, it clicks.

When life changes, adjust the budget. A new baby, a move, or a job change all require adjustments.

BEGINNER BUDGET EXAMPLE

INCOME

Paycheck 1	$2,000
Paycheck 2	$2,000
Total Income	$4,000

EXPENSES

Rent	$1,200
Groceries	$500
Car Payment	$350
Car Insurance	$150
Utilities	$200
Fun Money	$200
Debt Payments	$600
Other	$0
Total Expenses	$3,200
Leftover	$800

Think of this as your money snapshot. Write down your paychecks, list your bills, and see what's left. Don't overthink it. If you're not sure where something belongs, create its own line or list under "Other."

BUDGETING WHEN MARRIED

Money is one of the biggest reasons couples fight. Some studies rank it as the second leading cause of divorce, behind infidelity. And it's rarely about how much they make.

If you're older, already established, or bringing kids or significant assets into the marriage, it can make sense to keep certain accounts separate. However, for couples starting out early and still building their financial foundation, splitting everything usually makes life harder.

When you combine finances, things become clearer. You see exactly what's coming in and going out. You're forced to plan goals together. You stop running separate pots which compete and see how each person handles money. A shared budget shows those habits fast, so you can build one plan that works.

So why do many couples resist? The biggest reason is independence. People don't want to feel policed on every purchase. One partner orders Amazon and gets anxious. The other buys a new tool and feels judged. Keeping everything separate creates yours versus mine tension, misaligned goals, and financial secrets.

Research backs this up. A 2023 study from the University of Kansas found that couples who combined accounts reported higher trust and satisfaction in the first two years of marriage compared to those who kept money separate. They also showed more alignment on long-term goals.

The solution is to combine your money, then create room to operate. Pool your income, set shared goals, and talk about the big stuff early, like five-year direction, car plans, and retirement. When you agree on the vision, the numbers become a shared plan.

Then you add a pressure valve. Each partner gets their own fun money, no questions asked. You don't have to justify every purchase. It's already accounted for.

I also recommend a joint household miscellaneous category for random shared expenses. Decide in advance what counts as personal and what counts as household so you're not debating it later. Decide whether personal money carries over or resets, then stick to that rule.

My wife and I combined our finances after we got married, but we each have our own fun money line item. I don't usually spend much, but when I do, it comes in bursts.

One day I found a Nickelodeon Time Blaster alarm clock on eBay. As a kid, I always wanted one but never got it. Price: $120. When my wife realized I was buying it, she tried to talk me out of it. Then she shrugged, because it was my line item to spend. That's the deal. Our son loves it and still hits the demo button constantly.

It's ridiculous, but that's the point of fun money. Without it, this would have turned into an argument. With it, the budget worked and the bigger plan stayed intact.

BUDGET MYTHS THAT KEEP PEOPLE STUCK

"Budgeting means I can't have fun."

No. Budgeting is how you make room for fun without damaging next week's plan. Write down how much you want to spend on fun.

"I make too much money to need a budget."

In *Goldman Sach's 2025 Retirement Survey & Insights Report*, 40% of respondents making over $300,000 a year reported they are living paycheck to paycheck. The more you make, the more you need to plan for it. A bigger income also means the bigger the risk of waste. A budget protects it.

"I will budget when I get in a better place."

No. You get to a better place by budgeting. Write down your income and three bills. That's a budget. Begin with the essentials and add the rest later.

"It's too complicated."

List what comes in and what goes out. You don't need to be a master at spreadsheets or have a finance degree, but it does require paying attention. Grab a sheet of paper. Income at the top, bills underneath. That's a budget.

WHERE BUDGETS BREAK

Most budgets fall apart because of the stuff people should have seen coming. The Consumer Financial Protection Bureau found that 40% of families are hit by irregular expenses each year which push them into credit card debt.

Think of car maintenance, vet visits, holiday travel, or annual HOA dues. If it comes up once or twice a year, it belongs in your plan.

Gallup polling shows that only about 40% of Americans use a household budget. That means most people are flying blind with their money. It's no wonder the American Psychological Association reports that nearly two-thirds of adults say money is a significant source of stress in their lives. Most of the stress comes from not seeing what's already on the way. A budget gives you a clear view of what's coming due. It doesn't erase the bills, but it does erase the chaos.

That dinner out or those new shoes stop feeling like mistakes because you have planned for them. Instead of asking "Can I afford this?", you can say "I budgeted for this." That small shift makes spending feel planned instead of reckless.

The next chapter separates flexible spending from expenses that cannot be skipped or guessed. This is where your budget stops being a list and starts becoming a control system. Once those anchors are set, spending without guilt becomes automatic.

REMEMBER THIS

- A budget puts you in control.
- List your income and expenses, and give each dollar a job.
- Plan for irregular bills that blindside most people.
- Fun money and a household pot prevent fights.
- A budget removes guilt because it's part of the plan.

CHAPTER 6

THE NON-NEGOTIABLES

In 2022, Jackson, Mississippi lost its water system because the city had been running it on equipment far past its service life. Officials knew it. Engineers warned for years that the treatment plants and pumps needed replacement and routine maintenance. The costs were predictable and unavoidable.

Then a heavy rainstorm hit. It was the kind of storm the system had handled many times before. This time the worn-out pumps and controls couldn't keep up. Pressure collapsed across the city. Large neighborhoods lost clean water. Some had none at all. Schools closed. Restaurants shut down. Hospitals hauled in water just to stay open. The final bill for crisis repairs was far higher than the routine work that had been skipped for years.

It looked sudden, but it wasn't. The failure was the cost of ignoring known needs.

Households break the same way. If you don't save for the next repair or replacement, the bill still comes. It just shows up at the worst time.

THE WATER HEATER THAT WAITED TO STRIKE

When we bought our 16-year-old house, it still had the original water heater. It worked fine and passed inspection, but the average water heater only lasts about 10- to 15-years. I knew it was on borrowed time.

We started a sinking fund right away. I looked up the cost, divided it by 12, and set that amount aside each month. My plan was to be fully funded within a year.

But the water heater kept running. One year passed. Then two. And then one afternoon, I opened the door to my garage and saw what looked like the Fountains of Bellagio on full display. The tank had finally let go.

I shut off the water and power to the heater, called the plumber, and wrote a check the next day for a brand-new unit.

I had planned for this. The money was already set aside. It turned what could have been a panic moment into a routine repair.

You can't predict the moment something will break, but you can remove the financial worry ahead of time. In short: fund it before it fails.

STEP ONE: SPOT THE LANDMINES

Think through the expenses you know are coming in the near and medium term. Start with the big categories. These are recurring costs that show up again and again, whether you plan for them or not.

- Home maintenance and repairs like water heaters, roofs, and HVAC systems
- Annual renewals like insurance premiums, memberships, and school fees
- Gifts and holidays such as Christmas, birthdays, and graduations
- Vacations or weekend trips you have planned
- Big-ticket upgrades such as phones, laptops, furniture, and appliances
- Vet bills

These are the costs people pretend are surprises. The only surprise is being unprepared.

A quick example: Christmas catches people off guard even though it arrives the same day every year. The average American spends over $1,000 on gifts, parties, and travel. A large share lands on credit cards. When you finally start putting $50 a month aside in January, Christmas turns from a month breaker into a holiday you can actually enjoy.

Christmas is obvious. Home maintenance is quiet but bigger. Average home maintenance runs about 1% of a home's value each year. On a $250,000 house, that's $2,500. Without a plan, people swipe cards, drain savings, or take on payment plans when repairs hit.

Pet owners know the risk too. The American Pet Products Association reports that an emergency vet visit can run from $800 to $1,500. Without a plan, a lot of people end up financing it with a credit card or CareCredit.

SEP TWO: BREAK IT DOWN (AND BUILD A BUFFER)

Large costs look big until you turn them into monthly numbers.

Take the total and divide it by the number of months you have to save.

- $1,200 for a vacation next year? Save $100 a month
- $600 for Christmas? Start in January, that's $50 a month
- $800 for new tires? Spread over 12 months, that's about $67 a month

One year, we knew new tires were coming for my car. Instead of waiting for the bill to drop, we started a "tires" sinking fund at $70 a month. By the time we needed them, the money was ready. Extra cash never ruins a plan, but running short will.

STEP THREE: MOVE THE MONEY OR LOSE IT

Don't leave your sinking fund money sitting in your checking account. Set up a separate savings account (or a few) and move the money there.

Many online banks let you create sub-savings or "buckets" to stay organized. Name them. Fund them. Forget about them until you need them.

We learned this after trying to "just track it mentally." The money vanished into weekend trips and dinners out. Once we opened separate buckets, the money finally stayed put.

Your numbers won't be perfect at first. Sinking funds are flexible. You can increase or decrease them as life changes. Adjusting keeps you moving. Quitting resets the whole system.

WHY MOST PEOPLE FAIL WITHOUT SINKING FUNDS

Here's what usually happens:

- Swiping the card "just this once" and paying interest for months
- Fighting about money because nobody agrees what the budget can handle
- Feeling guilty spending on fun even when they need a break

Sinking funds remove guilt and keep you from undoing your progress with another round of debt. Without them, you react. With them, you're in control.

START SMALL, AVOID MISTAKES

If the whole list feels overwhelming, don't start with ten sinking funds. Start with one.

Pick Christmas or a new phone. Put $20 a month toward it and expand later.

Avoid the most common beginner mistakes:

- Starting too many funds at once and spreading yourself too thin
- Guessing too low and quitting instead of adjusting
- Leaving money in checking where it disappears into random spending

The amount matters less than building the habit. Once you plan ahead for one major cost, you won't run your budget any other way.

HOW IT LOOKS IN REAL LIFE

Here is how a few sinking funds might look in practice:

- New Laptop: $600/12 months = $50/month
- New iPhone: $800/12 months = about $67/month
- Car Insurance: $1,200/12 months = $100/month

Once you get the hang of it, many sinking funds stretch out over longer time frames. That means smaller monthly amounts and more breathing room in your budget. The planning gets easier the longer you stick with it.

A POSITIVE WIN: THE PAID-FOR VACATION

Sinking funds aren't only for hits. They also cover things you want.

One year we planned a family vacation. We decided on the cost, divided it by twelve, and saved for it each month. By the time the trip came, the money was sitting in its own account. We paid cash for the flights, the hotel, and the food.

The difference was immediate. No guilt and no second-guessing. No "we'll pay this off later." We actually enjoyed the vacation because the money stress was gone. That's what sinking funds give you. Protection and room to say yes without pressure.

We kept this vacation fund going so every future trip could feel the same way, paid for, with no guilt and no stress.

THE REAL PAYOFF

The payoff is control. When you fund known costs ahead of time, nothing in your month breaks when the bill hits. You absorb it and keep moving. That stability builds on itself.

When you don't plan, the same bills hit like a crisis. They pull cash out of your emergency fund, push balances onto cards, and create damage far bigger than the expense itself. That pattern doesn't stop on its own. It stops when you build margin.

You already know the next repair, replacement, or renewal is coming. Set up one sinking fund now and remove the risk before it becomes another hit.

REMEMBER THIS

- Christmas comes every year. It's not a surprise.
- Break big bills into small monthly bites.
- If it stays in checking, it's gone.
- Quitting keeps you broke. Adjusting keeps you moving.
- One sinking fund is enough to get started.

CHAPTER 7

INTENTIONAL, NOT RESTRICTIVE

I was at the dealership recently getting my oil changed when I noticed a salesman working the waiting room. He'd stop at each person and tell them their car was in great shape. Then he'd casually add that the dealership had demand for that model and would ask if he could give them a trade-in quote. Most people smiled and said yes.

I overheard an older couple talking about how if they could get a good deal, maybe it was worth it. Another man even went to test drive a redesigned SUV.

They all showed up for a $60 oil change, but he was planting the seed for a $40,000 purchase. You could see them warming up to an idea they didn't have when they woke up that morning.

Then he approached me. "Are you Josh?" I said yes.

Then he went into his pitch. "Your Accord has low miles for its year, and we have people looking for a used one like yours. It's in great shape. I think we could get you a strong trade-in number. Want to see what we could offer?"

"No. I'm good, thanks."

He smirked. "Driving it until the wheels fall off, huh?"

"No. I committed myself to 10 years with this one. I still have a few left."

He realized it wasn't going anywhere and moved on. If you don't control your decisions, the world will. This chapter gives you the filters that put you back in charge.

THE SPENDING FILTERS

The first is the 24-Hour Rule. If you see something you want, don't buy it right away. Keep a mental note or take a screenshot, then wait a day. That pause is often enough to separate a real want from a passing impulse.

The second is the Time Scale. Wait a day for small stuff. Wait a week for gadgets. Wait a month for anything over $1,000. Time exposes whether the purchase actually matters.

The third is the Trade-Off Test. Write down three things you really care about and three you don't. Put your money behind the first list. Be ruthless with the second.

The last is the Value Filter. Whenever possible, buy used or refurbished. You're paying the already depreciated price instead of the premium for new packaging.

WHY THE VALUE MINDSET WORKS

Sales signs, countdown timers, and low-stock warnings are designed to create urgency. That urgency speeds decisions up before you've thought them through. Your brain rewards fast action, even when the purchase wasn't planned. The feeling fades quickly. The spending doesn't.

I worked the electronics counter at Kmart in high school. One night, on the last day of a sale, a customer tried to buy a boombox. When I rang her up, her card was declined. Instead of walking away, she put the boombox on layaway. The urgency made the decision for her.

According to LendingTree, the average American spends over $300 a month on impulse purchases. That's more than $3,600 a year. Over a decade, it adds up to about $36,000, often without a clear memory of where it went.

Over time, that kind of spending changes what people can afford later.

THE POWER OF PATIENCE

Brian, a coworker of mine, became frustrated with his phone and walked into an Apple store to buy a brand-new iPhone. Two weeks later, someone mentioned that a newer model was dropping the next month. He had paid full price. The mistake wasn't the phone. It was buying without checking the timing.

I've made a similar mistake.

During COVID lockdowns, I decided to try photography as a new hobby. I bought a mirrorless camera bundle and convinced myself this was something I would stick with. The camera was powerful, but it was complicated, bulky, and frustrating to use. The fun faded fast.

Before my honeymoon, I picked up a cheap digital camera. It was automatic, easy to carry, and did exactly what I wanted. I enjoyed using it more than the expensive camera I had talked myself into.

A few years later, I sold both at a small loss. Buying used kept the damage minor, but patience would have kept me from making the mistake at all.

FOCUS ON WHAT YOU ACTUALLY VALUE

If you are passionate about travel but couldn't care less what you drive, spend less on the car and funnel that money into trips. If you love concerts but don't care about name-brand clothes, flip it.

Every dollar you give to something you don't value is a dollar stolen from something you do.

When my family had the choice, we kept driving the same car for years. It wasn't glamorous, but that trade-off bought us experiences we still remember. We could have upgraded the car. Instead, we upgraded our life.

USED IS UNDERRATED

Buying used is one of the most underrated money moves you can make.

According to SmartAsset, some of the best items to buy secondhand include cars, books, furniture, tools, baby gear, kids' clothing, exercise equipment, and video games.

If you refuse to even consider used, you're paying a sucker's tax. You're paying extra for nothing.

I bought exercise equipment on Facebook Marketplace in like-new condition for a third of the price, and I use it all the time. People often buy expensive equipment, use it for two weeks, and never touch it again.

ONE OF THE EASIEST WINS

One of the easiest ways to save big while still getting quality is through refurbished or open-box deals. Amazon calls it Renewed. Best Buy calls theirs Open Box. Many other stores have their own version.

Savings often run 20% to 50%, sometimes more. And the products usually come with the same warranty. RefurbMe reports that refurbished tech often goes through stricter testing than new.

I built my home office this way. I bought a refurbished monitor for 40% off, a keyboard through Amazon Warehouse for half price, and my speakers used off eBay for less than half the cost new. It looks brand new, works flawlessly, and cost me hundreds less because I chose to buy smart instead of buying fast.

Here is a quick Renewed Routine. Check the refurbished section before you buy new. Look at the warranty coverage. Test it at home. If it doesn't hold up, return it.

THE WAKE-UP CALL

Think about your own house. The treadmill that turned into a coat rack. The drawer full of gadgets that all have dead batteries.

A 2023 Movinga study found that 82% of the clothing Americans own hasn't been worn in the past year. That money is sitting in closets instead of buying anything useful.

Now imagine the opposite. Picture five years of buying with intention. No closet full of regrets. No piles of unused gear. Instead, you have a savings account that actually grows. You pay cash for the trip you want. You replace your car without a loan. Every purchase is guilt-free because you planned it.

Bankrate found that more than half of Americans regret at least one purchase from the past year. Usually, it was something bought on impulse.

Decide today that every dollar is a tool. Decide you will buy what matters and cut what doesn't. Decide you won't waste another year funding someone else's marketing tricks.

THE 30-DAY DECISION CHALLENGE

Talking about change does nothing. Action is what changes your life. For the next 30 days, run every purchase through one test: does this matter to me, or am I just reacting to a sale, an ad, or someone else's life?

If it matters, buy it with confidence. If it doesn't, walk away. Keep a simple list of what you almost bought and how much you saved.

At the end of the month, add it up. Most people are shocked. A few skipped lunches out, a couple of impulse clicks avoided, and suddenly you have a few hundred extra dollars sitting in your account.

Money doesn't disappear. You spend it, and someone else has it now.

REMEMBER THIS

- Impulse spending beats willpower. A system beats both.
- The wait is where the savings live.
- The first buyer pays for the box. You pay for the value.

CHAPTER 8

BREAKING THE CAR-PAYMENT CURSE

Car payments are treated as a normal expense. They tie up part of your income in something that loses value every month and offers no exit until the contract ends. Because the payment feels manageable, most people accept it without questioning the long-term consequences. This chapter breaks that default assumption.

The numbers show how common this has become. LendingTree's 2025 auto debt report puts the average new car payment at $745 a month. For used cars, it's $521. The average loan balance is $41,720 for new and $26,144 for used. As of 2025, 81% of new car purchases were financed.

The average new car now costs $49,000. That's 75% of what the average American makes in a year.

Depreciation makes it worse. The average new car loses about 30% of its value in the first two years and roughly 55% in the first five. You're paying top dollar for something that's worth less every time you drive it.

And those are just averages. Some models hold their value while others drop like a rock. For example, a Toyota 4Runner starts around $42,000 and is worth about $25,000 five years later. An Infiniti QX80 starts near $84,000 and is worth only about $29,000 after five years.

A car payment eats more of the average paycheck than a retirement contribution, college fund, or an extra mortgage payment. It's a direct blocker to building wealth.

THE MONTHLY PAYMENT MIRAGE

Walk into almost any dealership and the first thing they will ask is not, "What's your budget?" It's "What monthly payment are you looking for?"

Say you want a $25,000 car. At 5% interest over 60 months, the payment lands at $472 a month. If the salesperson convinces you that you can handle $600 a month, you could walk out spending nearly $8,000 more without noticing, just because you focused on the monthly payment.

If you stretch the loan to 72 months or more, which is now common, it gets even worse. The longer the term, the lower the monthly number looks, and the easier it is to get tricked into overspending by thousands.

When you sit down to finalize the deal, you may see a four-square worksheet. It's a game where they juggle price, trade-in, down payment, and term until the payment looks comfortable. It's designed to distract you from the total cost. Stick to your out-the-door worksheet. If numbers change or new charges appear, stop them and make them explain every line before you sign.

Dealers have recently gone viral on social media, posting videos of coworkers rattling off sky-high payments to make debt feel normal. The goal isn't to help you budget. It's about making lifelong debt feel ordinary.

RENT WITH RIMS

Leasing can look appealing. You get a smaller payment and a shiny new car every few years, but for most people, it's the most expensive way to "own" a vehicle.

You're paying to borrow something you will never own. The average lease payment in 2025 was over $600 a month. That's $7,200 a year, gone forever. It feels easy, but it keeps you in payments forever.

One friend of mine turned his car in and was hit with $1,200 in penalties for mileage and bald tires. Three years of payments plus fees and he had nothing to show for it.

YOUR LAST CAR PAYMENT

Escaping car payments doesn't mean driving a beater or giving up nice cars forever. It's making one smart purchase, keeping it long enough to save for the next one in cash, and never signing another car note again.

I call it *Your Last Car Payment.* You buy once, you keep it, and from then on, you're free.

A lot of people upgrade because they want to look the part. They want the latest model in their driveway, something that looks good at work or in front of neighbors, but nobody would be impressed by your payment history. People are impressed by those who actually have money. Trying to look rich is the fastest way to stay broke.

Another excuse is fear of repairs. Trading a car every few years just guarantees you will always have payments. AAA estimates it costs $12,297 a year to own a new car in 2025. That number assumes five years of ownership and driving 15,000 miles a year. That includes depreciation, higher insurance, and financing fees. A reliable used car that kept up with routine maintenance will almost always have lower ownership costs.

Finally, there's herd mentality. Most people you know will always have a car payment and are vocal about it. That's why so many believe it's normal. If you do what everyone else does, you will get what everyone else has: stress, debt, and no progress.

I'm not saying you should hate cars. I love cars. I go to the auto show every year, but I had to separate that enjoyment from my finances. When you tie your self-worth to what you drive, the dealer wins.

THE CHECKLIST THAT BREAKS THE CYCLE

Here's the framework for making it happen. Whether the car you pick is simple or a little nicer, the rules don't change.

1. **Proven reliability.** Buy a model known to last. Brands like Toyota and Honda often make it to 200,000 miles without major problems. Ignore this part and the whole plan falls apart.
2. **Comfort matters.** If you hate your car, you will replace it early. Pick something you actually like so you stay out of the showroom.
3. **Economical to run.** It needs to be affordable to maintain and have low depreciation.
4. **An 8-year mindset.** 8 years is where you feel the payoff. If you can stretch it to 10, even better. That is where the math flips and you start banking real money.
5. **Pay it off in 3 years or less.** If it takes longer, you locked yourself into too long of payments. Two years is even better.

But what if a dealer waves 0% financing at you or a luxury model is on special? The cars with the lowest depreciation are almost never the luxury models, and 0% still locks you into years of payments.

HOW I BROKE FREE

When I decided to get out of the cycle, I didn't have the cash to buy outright. I knew if I didn't do this right, I'd be stuck with payments for another five years.

The model I wanted was listed at $32,000. I negotiated it down to $29,800, but I felt there was still room so I expanded my search to prior-year inventory and found one with just 47 miles on the odometer. I ended up paying $27,300. That move alone cut out the steepest year of depreciation.

I financed only what I had to and used the same payoff strategies from Step 2. The loan was gone in 18 months. Every month without a payment felt like I was finally getting ahead, and that momentum made it easier to keep pushing.

Once the note was paid off, I shifted to the next step. I started a sinking fund for my next car. I calculated what a future replacement might cost in 8 or 9 years and overshot my savings goal. I ignored trade-in value so I knew I could pay cash no matter what.

Would I do it exactly the same way today? Probably not. I would look hard at certified pre-owned. CPO vehicles have already taken their biggest depreciation hit. They go through strict manufacturer-backed inspections and many come with longer warranties than the new models.

You can win either way, but CPO often works out better with a lower price, proven reliability, and more peace of mind.

PAYMENT PRISON VS CASH FREEDOM

Chris keeps a car payment for life. 20 years of $745 payments adds up to almost $180,000 gone. At the end, all he has is another car that keeps losing value.

Alex does it differently. He pays off his car in 18 months, and drives it for a total of 10 years. During those payment-free years, he saves the same $745 every month. When it's time for the next car, he has about $75,000 set aside. He buys a $50,000 car in cash and still has $25,000 left.

He keeps saving after that. Even if he earns 0% on that money, after 20 years Alex owns his car and has over $100,000 in cash.

With the car payment gone, one of the biggest monthly drains is removed. The next step is making sure your housing decision doesn't recreate the same trap on a larger scale. A paid-off car gives you flexibility most people never get. The next chapter shows how to use that flexibility without letting a house payment undo it.

REMEMBER THIS

- A car payment is the slow bleed that keeps you broke.
- Dealers push monthly payments to hide the real cost.
- Leasing is renting. You pay more and own nothing.
- Your car doesn't define you. Keep your money instead of payments.
- Pay it off fast, keep it long, and send the payment to yourself.

CHAPTER 9

HOW TO BUY THE HOUSE AND KEEP YOUR LIFE

The easiest way to become house poor is to buy near the top of what the bank approves. What comes next is predictable. You save for the down payment, get pre-approved, and work with a recommended realtor. After all the bank's questions, the document uploads, and the income verification, it's easy to assume the number means it's safe.

Then the hidden costs start stacking up. HOA hikes. Insurance jumps. Constant maintenance. Each one nibbles away until there's nothing left for the life you thought the house would support. What was supposed to feel like security now creates constant pressure.

That pressure has a name - house poor.

This chapter shows how people walk into it, why banks don't stop it, and how to buy a house that supports your life instead of shrinking it.

WHY PEOPLE END UP HOUSE POOR

Bank math says you can make the payment. Life math includes ER visits and braces.

Take Laura. She earned $95,000 and bought at the top of her approval. Her $2,700 payment took 38% of her take-home pay, and within a year, surprise repairs were going on credit cards. She wasn't broke. She was house poor.

The bank made sure she could make the payment. The realtor helped her find a house she liked. Protecting her lifestyle was never part of either job.

A STARTER HOME IS A TOOL

When I bought my first house, money was tight. It was a 2-bedroom, 2-bath townhouse with 1,000 square feet. I used down payment assistance from my local housing authority because I didn't have much saved. It wasn't my dream home, and it certainly wasn't a status symbol.

The value went up over time. That house acted as a forced savings account and made the next move possible.

Realistic options still exist if you treat housing like a financial choice instead of a personal statement. The concept of a forever home is a trap. You need a home you can afford without it squeezing your life.

QUICK GUT CHECK: ARE YOU ALREADY HOUSE POOR?

Here's a 30-second gut check: Add up your mortgage payment plus HOA. Divide that by your take-home pay, then multiply by 100. The tipping point is 30%. Above that, you'll start making sacrifices. Over 35% puts you in the danger zone.

For example, if you bring home $6,000 a month and your total payment is $2,200, that is 37%. That's well past safe and squarely in house-poor territory.

THE MORTGAGE RAMP

So how do you buy a house without letting it steal your life? You climb *The Mortgage Ramp*.

Think of your mortgage like a ramp. The steeper it is, the faster you reach the top, which is debt-free living. The flatter the ramp, the longer you drag it out and the more interest you hand to the bank.

This is where the mortgage stops feeling heavy and starts working for you:

- **20-Year at 30% (Under 50):** If you're under 50, a 20-year fixed-rate mortgage at no more than 30% of your take-home pay is the right entry point. The payment is manageable, and the lower rate keeps more of your money going toward equity instead of interest.

- **15-Year at 28% (50+):** Income growth generally slows in your 50s, so you want the faster payoff working in your favor. A 15-year fixed-rate mortgage at no more than 28% of your take-home pay keeps you ahead without straining your month. You save a huge chunk on interest and open up cash flow years earlier.

Both 15- and 20-year loans come with lower interest rates than a 30-year, so you pay less to the bank from day one.

Here's what the math looks like on a $250,000 mortgage at 6%:

- A 30-year costs about $290,000 in interest.
- A 20-year cuts that to about $180,000.
- A 15-year cuts it to about $130,000.

That is a $110,000 difference between the 20-year and the 30-year loan.

REAL WORLD TIMING

According to *Redfin*, the median first-time homebuyer is now 38. Data from *The Zebra* and *Redfin News* show most people will stay in those homes for 12 to 13 years before moving again.

People are also expected to work longer than past generations. Surveys from *Gallup* and *Transamerica* show many younger workers expect to retire closer to 68 or 70, and some plan to keep working part time even longer. People are living longer and staying healthier.

Even with the late start, this ramp still gives you a path to pay off your home before you retire. A 20-year mortgage earlier in life builds equity faster and gives you room to adapt if things change or you decide to move. On a 30-year mortgage, it takes about 10 years before a meaningful amount of your payment starts going toward equity instead of interest.

CASE STUDY: MAX AND SARAH'S MORTGAGE CHOICES

Max and Sarah are 32, both teachers. Between coaching, summer school, and extra duties, their income totals $140,000. They save 15% for retirement and max out their family HSA. Their take-home pay, after taxes, FICA, retirement contributions, HSA, and health insurance premiums, is about $6,675 a month. That is the money actually hitting their bank account each month.

They are buying a $223,500 home with a $201,150 mortgage. Because they are putting down only 10%, they pay private mortgage insurance (PMI) of about $120 a month, until they reach 20% equity. Escrow for taxes and homeowners insurance, plus HOA dues, adds another $500 a month.

- **30-Year Loan at 5.75% interest:** The base loan payment is about $1,174 a month, plus $120 PMI and $500 escrow and HOA, for a total of **$1,794 (27% of take-home)**. After five years, they have built about $36,900 in equity. PMI would last close to 10-years.

- **20-Year Loan at 5.5% interest:** The base loan payment is about $1,384 a month, plus $120 PMI and $500 escrow and HOA, for a total of **$2,004 (30% of take-home)**. After five years, they have built about $54,200 in equity. PMI drops in about six years.

- **15-Year Loan at 5.1% interest:** The base loan payment is about $1,601 a month, plus $120 PMI and $500 escrow and HOA, for a total of **$2,221 (33% of take-home)**. After five years, they own about $73,200 of their home. PMI disappears in under four years.

That's a $17,300 gap in equity in only five years between the 20-year and the 30-year.

For teachers like Max and Sarah, the 20-year loan is the right balance. It builds real equity, kills PMI sooner, and fits their budget without strain.

Equity Built After 5 & 10 Years with $201,150 Mortgage

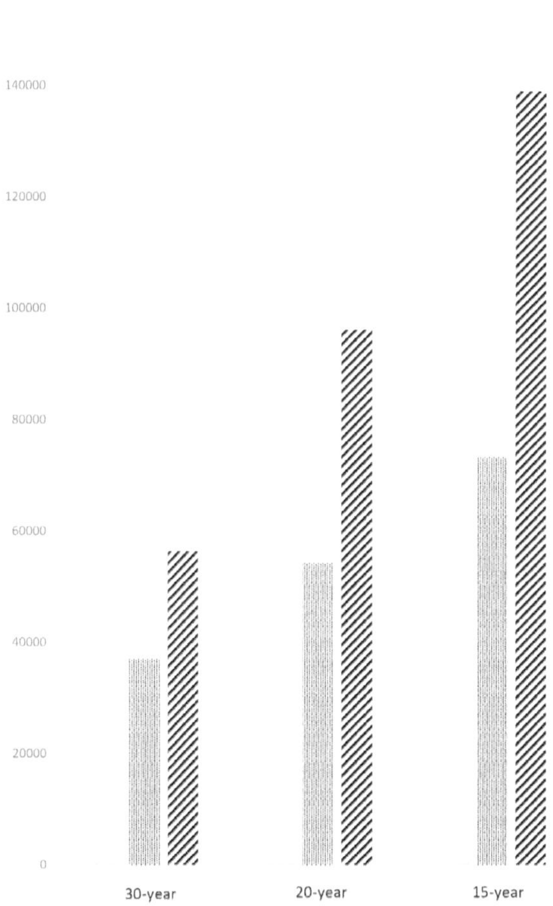

PAYING IT OFF EARLY

Once you have the right mortgage, make it disappear faster.

Here are the simplest ways to pay it off early:

- **Divide by 12:** Take your monthly principal and interest, divide it by 12, and add that amount each month. You're effectively making one extra payment a year without feeling the hit all at once.
- **Use windfalls:** Tax refunds, bonuses, or extra income from side work.
- **Keep raises in check:** When your income goes up, put part of the difference toward the principal.

Extra payments kill interest fast. One extra month today can wipe out multiple months later.

On a 30-year, $250,000 mortgage at 6%, an extra $200 a month cuts almost five years off the loan and saves over $50,000 in interest.

MORTGAGE BASICS YOU ACTUALLY NEED TO KNOW

Think of a mortgage as having three main parts: the term, the interest-rate type, and the loan program.

The term is how long you will be making payments, usually 8, 10, 15, 20, or 30 years. The 30-year is the default for most people because it comes with the smallest monthly payment, but there's a catch. It builds equity very slowly. Mortgages are amortized, which means your early payments are mostly interest. On a $300,000 mortgage at 6.5%, you would have about $19,000 of equity after five years, only 6.4%. On a 15-year loan at 6%, you would have almost $72,000 in equity, about 24%.

Interest rates can be fixed or adjustable. A fixed rate never changes, which makes it simple and predictable. An adjustable-rate mortgage (ARM) starts with a lower rate for a few years, then the rate can adjust every year, subject to a cap. It might start cheaper than a fixed loan, but if rates go up, your payment can jump.

Last is the loan program. These programs exist for different situations, and there's criteria to qualify for them. Conventional loans are for borrowers with good credit and steady income. FHA loans, backed by the Federal Housing Administration, allow smaller down payments but have extra insurance costs. VA loans are for veterans and active-duty military. USDA loans are for rural areas and have income limits. Jumbo loans are for properties above standard lending limits.

THE MYTH: "NEVER PAY OFF YOUR MORTGAGE EARLY"

One of the most common things you'll hear is that you should never pay off your mortgage early. The argument sounds convincing. Instead of sending extra money to the bank, you could invest it, earn a higher return, and come out ahead. Or you could park it in a high-yield savings account and keep flexibility.

In theory, this works. If the market performed well, you could end up with more wealth than if you had paid off the house. Other than the so-called lost decade from 2000 to 2009, history shows you likely would have come out ahead. However, future returns aren't guaranteed, and that assumes you invest every dollar and leave it untouched for decades, which most people don't do.

Real life happens. Over time, lifestyle creep takes over. A little upgrade here, new subscriptions there, and suddenly those investment dollars are buying a nicer car or paying for a trip. The long-term plan gets eaten by short-term habits.

My survey of 400 homeowners showed this clearly. Over half admitted dipping into their "invest the difference" money for vacations, cars, and other expenses long before it could grow.

Even if you did invest it all, you still have to account for taxes. Stock gains are taxed when you sell, but interest from a high-yield savings account is taxed every year it's earned. That 3% you make in a HYSA is not really 3% after taxes.

By comparison, every extra dollar you put toward your mortgage is a guaranteed return equal to your interest rate, and that benefit isn't taxed. Because mortgages are amortized, extra principal payments have a compounding effect. They reduce future interest charges and shorten your payoff, which steadily increases your net worth.

Before you start paying extra on your mortgage, you should be out of all other debt, have a fully funded emergency fund, be saving for your kid's education if that's a goal, and be adequately funding your retirement and other sinking funds. Only then does it make sense to use extra money to pay your home off early.

THE BOTTOM LINE

Your mortgage shouldn't run your life. Pick the right size, lock the right term, and pay it down with purpose. That way you own your home and your margin.

Most people say they will invest the difference. My survey of 400 homeowners showed most couldn't stick with it.

What happens after the purchase matters more than the purchase itself. The next chapter looks at what homeowners actually do once the payment is locked in. This is where good intentions break down and where most long-term outcomes are decided. Understanding that gap is what keeps your house from becoming another financial trap.

REMEMBER THIS

- Over 35% of your take-home pay means you're house poor.
- The Mortgage Ramp is the safest way to buy and pay off a home.
- A 20-year loan is the right balance for most people.
- A 15-year loan saves the most if the payment fits your life.
- Banks don't set your limits. You do.

CHAPTER 10

WE ASKED 400 HOMEOWNERS: HERE'S WHAT THEY REALLY DID

More than half of homeowners who invested extra money instead of paying down their mortgage ended up raiding their account.

That's the headline my survey uncovered. These were homeowners doing exactly what mainstream advice recommends. On paper, investing instead of paying down your house looks smart. In real life, most people don't stick with it long enough for it to work.

To see if this was routine, I surveyed over 400 homeowners who were making the minimum mortgage payment while investing extra money.

MOST PEOPLE RAID THE ACCOUNT

If you've ever invested extra money instead of putting it toward your mortgage, did you end up using any of that money?

54% said yes.

The goal was to come out ahead of the mortgage rate, but more than half ended up touching it. Some did it for emergencies. Others did it for big purchases.

This wasn't a one-off. Once people pull from an account, they tend to do it again. My survey showed that 87% of people who pulled from investments did so within the first five years. That's long before compounding ever has a chance to work.

Another 5% had done a cash-out refinance but said they never touched their investment money. A cash-out refinance is when you take a new, larger mortgage and pocket the difference in cash. That's technically true, but it still misses the point. They still turned their home equity into spending money. Both moves turn equity into cash.

When you add those together, about 59% of people who chose to invest over early payoff eventually tapped the money. 45% of people who didn't pull from the account admitted they came close.

And if anything, that number might be conservative. It doesn't include homeowners who took out a loan against their home equity, known as a Home Equity Line of Credit (HELOC). According to a nationwide survey from MeridianLink, nearly 30% of U.S. homeowners say they're considering taking out a HELOC within the next 12 months.

People take some out, tell themselves they'll put it back in, and usually don't. It happens faster than they expect.

THE PLAN COLLAPSES BY YEAR THREE

The strategy broke early. Homeowners who invested the extra money for less than 3 years were the most at risk. In fact, 75% of all withdrawals in the survey came from this group.

A family decides to invest $400 a month instead of paying down the mortgage. Two years in, the furnace breaks. They don't have enough in savings, so they pull from the brokerage account. A few months later, a car repair pops up. Then their child needs braces. By year three, the account often holds less than it did at the end of year one. They're leaving the account exposed.

That's why you need stability before anything else. Without that foundation, the strategy falls apart fast.

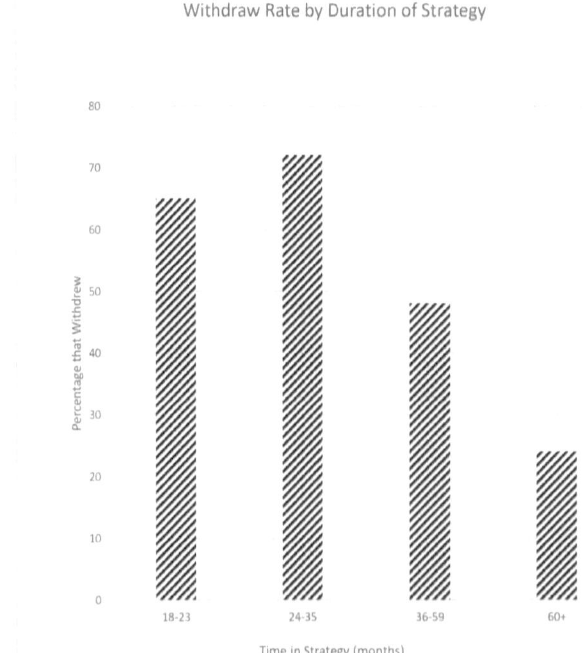

The timing of the withdrawals wasn't random. The biggest spike showed up in the 24-to-35-month range. I didn't ask what year people bought their homes, but that window lines up with the 2022 to early 2023 market peak. Prices were high, and inflation was running hot. Groceries, gas, and everyday bills were climbing fast. Interest rates were moving up too, which made mortgages, credit cards, and other debt more expensive. A lot of families who bought during that period were already stretched. When pressure hit, the investment account was the first place they turned.

SIX FIGURES, STILL NO CUSHION

Most people assume only lower-income families would cash out their investment accounts, but that wasn't always the case.

In many places, six figures is a solid income, but these people are still dipping into money they planned to leave invested.

Take a family earning $120,000. Their mortgage is $2,800, plus a $600 car loan and daycare at $1,500. It works until something breaks. A $5,000 HVAC bill or $2,500 ER visit, and the extra they've been investing becomes the bailout.

My survey showed that pattern again and again. These families had the income, but no cushion. No emergency fund means every problem hits harder.

INVESTMENTS BECAME THE BUFFER

The real failure showed up when the investment account became the buffer. They needed the money, and they pulled from it too early. Once that cycle starts, compounding never gets a chance to work.

In my survey, 64% of those who withdrew said they regretted it.

This is why an emergency fund isn't optional. It's the only thing that stands between your investments and the constant hits that show up over a normal year. Without cash reserves, people aren't really investing. They're just holding money until the next crisis empties it.

When pressure hits, avoiding an immediate loss feels more urgent than protecting future gains. Pulling from the investment account stops the pain right away. The cost shows up later, which makes the decision feel safer in the moment.

At the same time, money that looks available rarely stays untouched. Once investments become an option, it tends to get used.

So don't let your home be the excuse to stretch too far. And don't let "invest the spread" talk you into a mortgage that leaves no room for setbacks. Any plan that falls apart the first time life gets messy isn't worth following.

WHAT HAS TO BE TRUE

The math only works if the money stays untouched. In most households, it doesn't. Expenses rise. Repairs happen. The investment account turns into the backup plan, and at that point, the original plan is already gone.

This is where math meets real life. The next chapter shifts away from optimization and toward decisions that hold up when life gets messy. Progress only compounds when the structure can withstand pressure.

REMEMBER THIS

- Most people don't keep the money invested.
- The first 3 years decide everything. Most withdrawals happen before compounding has a chance.
- A six-figure paycheck still collapses without savings.
- No emergency fund means every problem hits your investments.
- Stability first. Growth second. That's the only plan that works.

CHAPTER 11

DIAPERS AND DEGREES

Most families don't get into trouble in one moment. It happens slowly, while everything still looks fine.

They buy a home that fits their plan. Two incomes cover the payment. The bills get paid. The budget works, but there isn't much room left. At the time, it feels normal.

Then kids arrive.

The costs aren't a surprise. Everyone knows children are expensive. Childcare, medical bills, food, school supplies, activities. They're the kinds of costs most families expect and plan around.

By the time those costs arrive, most of the big decisions are already locked in. Housing and cars are decided, and the rest of the budget follows. Retirement contributions slow down and savings get tapped. That's why even good incomes can feel tight for years.

You don't need to predict every phase. You need to move the adjustment earlier, before the pressure shows up.

START BUDGETING BEFORE THE BABY ARRIVES

If you're expecting a child or planning for one, start adjusting your budget now. Waiting until the expense shows up is what turns a predictable cost into pressure.

When we bought our house, we knew a family was in our future. We looked up the average cost of daycare, added about 20%, and put that amount toward our mortgage principal each month. It lowered our balance and forced us to live with the expense before it was required.

That amount doesn't have to go toward the mortgage. If you're building an emergency fund, saving for medical costs, or setting money aside for baby expenses, that works too. The point is making room before the cost arrives.

As of 2025, the average cost of daycare in the United States is about $15,500 a year. That figure is up 51% since 2023 and 282% since 1990. In many areas, it costs even more. Parents often expect relief once their child leaves the newborn room, but tuition increases usually erase it.

That cost often collides with housing. A 2024 Redfin survey found that about half of homeowners with children struggle to afford their housing payments. Housing and childcare tend to hit in the same window, after most of the budget is already spoken for.

SHOULD ONE OF YOU STAY HOME?

One of the biggest decisions families face is whether one parent should step out of the workforce. In the past, this choice was clearer because one partner usually earned much more. Today, that gap is smaller. A 2023 Pew Research study found that women aged 25-34 earn about 92% of what men earn.

For many families, both paychecks matter. Staying home isn't a lifestyle preference, it's a major financial hit. Leaving work cuts income, retirement contributions, raises, and long-term growth.

The pressure around this choice is real. Moms often feel it more, not because dads don't care, but because the expectation to do both still falls harder on women. The math stays the same either way.

Take a basic scenario. Two partners each earn $65,000. Together, that's $130,000. If one stops working, income drops by half. You also lose the 401k match, yearly raises, and future earning power. Over time, the gap can reach hundreds of thousands of dollars.

There isn't a universal right answer. What matters is understanding the trade-offs. If one parent stays home, plan for the income loss and long-term impact. If both continue working, plan for childcare and support costs. Make the decision with clarity and own it.

THE COSTS DON'T STOP AFTER DAYCARE

At some point, daycare ends. But don't expect a clean break. After-school care, summer camps, programs, and sports show up fast. You will feel relief when kindergarten starts, but the costs don't disappear.

A week of summer camp might run $400. Piano lessons might be $80 a month. Soccer fees, uniforms, and weekend travel stack up before you even realize it. It isn't as heavy as daycare, but you still feel it in the budget.

The only thing more expensive than daycare is pretending you can wing it. One of the best tools you can use while your children are still in daycare is the DCFSA.

FREE MONEY FOR CHILDCARE (DCFSA)

If your employer offers it, a Dependent Care Flexible Spending Account (DCFSA) lets you set aside up to $7,500 in pre-tax money each year for childcare. This includes daycare, preschool, summer camp, and before- or after-school care.

The money is use-it-or-lose-it within the calendar year. Unless your plan has a grace period, you must spend it by year-end. You'll need documentation from the provider such as receipts, tax ID numbers, and proof of service to qualify.

That $7,500 lowers more than your federal income taxes. It also reduces your payroll taxes including Social Security and Medicare, which together take 7.65% of most paychecks. In the 22% federal bracket, that is $2,224 in combined tax savings.

Enroll if you qualify. You're spending the money anyway. This helps you keep more of it.

THE COLLEGE FUND THAT PAYS YOU BACK (529 PLANS)

Most parents aren't ready for college costs. A 2023 Discover survey found that 70% of parents with college-bound kids worry they don't have enough saved.

A 529 plan lets you invest after-tax money into an account that grows tax-free as long as it's used for qualified education expenses. These include college tuition, books, fees, and sometimes room and board. Some states also give tax deductions or credits for contributing. The earlier you start, the more it grows. Time is the real advantage.

Each state runs its own version of the plan. The rules and benefits aren't the same everywhere, so take a quick look at what your state offers.

529 plans are flexible. If your child doesn't use all the money, you can transfer it to another family member or even save it for a future grandchild. That lets the money keep growing for decades. You can also use part of it to pay off student loans. And thanks to the SECURE Act 2.0, you can roll up to $35,000 of leftover 529 funds into a Roth IRA if certain conditions are met. Transfers to a relative may have gift tax implications, so talk to a tax advisor if you go that route.

What if you're starting late? Start with what you can. Every dollar you save now is one less your child needs to borrow later.

You can also check to see if your local community college has any programs. Some offer tuition reimbursement or even free tuition for graduates of nearby high schools, especially if they have lived in the district for several years. Two years at a community college can cut the cost of a degree in half or more. It also gives you a few extra years to save. It lowers the cost without limiting options.

For most families, a 529 is enough. Other options exist, but they usually add complexity or only make sense in narrow cases.

THE OTHER EDUCATION ACCOUNTS (MOSTLY MEH)

Coverdell Education Savings Accounts grow tax-free when used for qualified education expenses, including K-12 costs, but they come with a $2,000 annual contribution limit per child, income caps, and age restrictions. For most families, a 529 plan is simpler and more powerful.

Some states offer prepaid tuition plans that let you lock in today's tuition rates at public in-state universities. It might sound like a smart hedge against rising costs, but I don't recommend them. They typically only cover tuition, not books or housing, and they limit where your child can attend. If your child ends up going ineligible school or chooses a different path, the refund is often only your contributions. You trade flexibility for predictability, and most families don't come out ahead.

Custodial accounts, called UGMA or UTMA accounts, short for the Uniform Gifts to Minors Act and the Uniform Transfers to Minors Act, are another option. These accounts are flexible, and the money can be used for anything. The downside is that once your child turns 18 or 21, depending on your state, the money legally belongs to them. You also lose the tax advantages of a 529, and earnings are subject to kiddie-tax rules. These accounts can make sense for teaching investing or passing down wealth, but they are usually a poor fit for college savings.

TEACH THEM TO HANDLE MONEY

You can save every dollar they'll ever need, but it won't help if they don't know how to handle money when it's theirs.

Start early. Let them handle money in small doses. Take them to the store with their own spending cash. Let them choose. Let them make mistakes. If they spend it too fast and regret it, they learn from it.

Have them budget their allowance. Break it into spending, saving, and giving so they see the difference between fun, goals, and generosity. If they want something big like a PlayStation or a car, set up a matching system for it. For every dollar they save, you match a portion. They still do the work, but they get to see progress. That teaches them to save toward goals, and to think twice before buying the next upgrade.

Talk about what things cost and why you make certain choices. Let them hear you say, "We're not buying that today because we're saving for something else." Hearing your reasoning teaches more than a lecture will.

Kids learn what you model. If you spend intentionally, save on purpose, and give generously, you're already teaching them what matters.

As they grow, increase their responsibility. Let a teenager manage part of their clothing budget for the school year. If they spend it all early on one big purchase, they will see the impact of their choice.

And remember, it's fine to help your kids, just don't raise them to expect it. If they know you'll always bail them out, they'll never learn to stand on their own. Easy money removes the push to work.

DON'T PREDICT. PREPARE.

You can't predict every dollar or every turn. You'll never get it perfect. What you can do is prepare for where the pressure shows up.

Families don't fall behind because they missed some exact number. They fall behind because they waited too long to adjust.

Build margin early. Make room before the costs arrive. Don't rely on timing to save you.

Your kids won't know your exact budget, but they will remember if stress pulled your attention away from them.

REMEMBER THIS

- Prepare early. It costs less than fixing it later.
- Don't leave free money sitting on the table. Use the DCFSA and the 529.
- Small, steady deposits buy your kids real options.
- Teaching your kids to handle money matters more than saving it for them.
- Prediction doesn't help. Preparation does.

STEP 4:

PROTECT AND PREPARE

oney feels stable until the moment it doesn't. Most months look normal, then one event hits and exposes every weak spot in your system.

Protection is what stops that hit from turning into a setback that drags on for years. Insurance, health planning, and retirement saving are the controls that keep a household standing when the timing is bad.

Surprises never show up at a good time. They hit harder when you're not ready.

Retirement planning carries the same pattern. Delay pushes more weight onto the years ahead.

This step transfers the risks you can't afford to carry. You set up a way to handle medical costs without draining your savings and start retirement early so compound growth carries more of the load.

Protection stops you from losing ground now. Preparation keeps you steady later. You need both if you want your progress to hold.

CHAPTER 12

THE SAFETY NET NO ONE TALKS ABOUT

Everything you've done so far has been about moving forward. This step is about continuing that progress.

Insurance is easy to skip when nothing has gone wrong yet. It feels like a bill you can push off until later. Then something happens and you find out what you were really exposed to.

Maybe it's a car accident. Maybe it's a medical emergency. The details change, but the result is the same. The cost is bigger than the margin you've built.

This chapter is about protection. Coverage that can take a hit without undoing the work you've put in. The goal is simple. Cover the risks you actually face right now and ignore the junk.

AUTO INSURANCE

Auto insurance is one of the few coverages you're legally required to carry. Even though most drivers have it, many still overpay or leave themselves badly underinsured.

When you get a quote, the insurer or agent asks you which limits you want for each type of coverage.

Here's what you need to know.

LIABILITY COVERAGE

Liability coverage pays for damage or injuries you cause to others. This falls into two parts:

- Bodily injury (if you hurt someone)
- Property damage (if you hit their car, home, fence, etc.)

A common recommended limit is 100/300/100. That means up to $100,000 per person, $300,000 total per accident, and $100,000 for property damage.

Medical bills add up fast. So do luxury car repairs. A single accident can lead to a six-figure judgment. If your limits are too low, the insurance only pays up to that cap. Anything beyond it could put your assets at risk.

Many states only require minimum limits such as 25/50/25, or lower, but those numbers exist so you can legally drive, not so you're financially protected.

COMPREHENSIVE AND COLLISION

Comprehensive and collision sound like they go together, but they're actually two separate types of protection for your own vehicle.

- Comprehensive covers non-collision damage: theft, fire, hail, falling trees, vandalism, and animal hits.
- Collision covers damage to your car when you hit another car or object, regardless of who's at fault.

If your car is older and paid off, you might think about dropping these to save money, but if you can't afford to repair or replace your car out of pocket, keep them.

MEDICAL PAYMENTS/PIP

This kicks in fast and covers the first wave of medical costs for you and your passengers such as ER visits, X-rays, or surgery. In some states it's called MedPay. In others it's Personal Injury Protection, or PIP.

Limits are usually low, from $1,000 to $10,000, but they can help cover immediate costs no matter who's at fault.

UNINSURED AND UNDERINSURED MOTORIST COVERAGE (UM/UIM)

This is the coverage most people overlook, and it's where a lot of auto insurance plans fail.

If someone hits you and doesn't have insurance, or doesn't have enough of it, this coverage protects you. In 2023, an estimated 15.4% of drivers in the U.S. were uninsured. That means 1 in 6 drivers on the road could hit you and leave you footing the bill.

If there's no insurance or assets to collect from and you don't carry UM/UIM, there's no one left to pay. That's why you want limits that match your liability coverage.

RENTAL REIMBURSEMENT

If your household depends on one vehicle, don't skip rental reimbursement. This covers the cost of a rental car while yours is in the shop after a covered loss.

It's usually cheap, and if losing your only car would disrupt your life, it's worth every penny.

WHAT ABOUT GAP INSURANCE?

Gap insurance pays the difference between what you owe on your loan and what your car is worth if it's totaled out. It only exists because the loan outpaces the value of the car, which is a position you should work to exit quickly.

Bottom line: Don't overthink the add-ons, but don't carry the bare minimum coverage just because it's cheaper. The cost difference between low limits and adequate ones is small compared to what's exposed.

HEALTH INSURANCE

Medical bills are the number one cause of bankruptcy in America. Health insurance isn't a perk from work. It's protection against a financial hit that can undo years of progress. Skip it, and one ER visit can cost more than your car.

Hospitals are required to stabilize you in an emergency, but they aren't required to provide the follow-up care that helps you fully recover. That's why you need health insurance, even if you rarely see a doctor.

Most people get coverage through their employer, and the two main options are a Preferred Provider Organization (PPO) and high-deductible health plans (HDHP).

A PPO has higher monthly premiums but lower costs when you see the doctor. You'll often pay fixed copays for visits or prescriptions. An HDHP has much lower premiums but higher upfront costs. You pay the full bill until you meet your deductible, which can be several thousand dollars. This catches people off guard when a large bill shows up before they've built their buffer. After that, you only pay a small percentage of the bill. Preventive care such as annual checkups is generally covered under both.

For many families, the HDHP is the smarter play. Lower premiums let you keep more of your paycheck, and when you pair it with a Health Savings Account, you gain one of the most flexible ways to protect yourself now while building long-term savings you can use if larger medical costs show up later. If you have ongoing medical needs, frequent prescriptions, or you're planning a family, a PPO may make sense, but for most people, the HDHP is the long-term win.

Health insurance handles the immediate risk. An HSA helps you absorb the costs.

DISABILITY INSURANCE

The Social Security Administration estimates that one in four 20-year-olds today will face a long-term disability before retirement.

Most people think disability means a freak accident. In reality, it's usually illness, cancer, heart disease, and chronic back problems that stop people from working.

Short-term disability insurance typically lasts 3 to 6 months, though some plans extend up to a year, and it replaces about 60% of your paycheck. Many employers include it as a benefit. The bigger risk is what happens when that runs out and your income stops. That's where long-term disability insurance comes in. I've seen healthy people unable to work for months following a sudden event, and disability insurance is the only thing that kept their finances standing. It can cover you for years, sometimes until retirement, and it's the coverage most people don't have.

A diagnosis or chronic illness can erase your paycheck overnight. Your bills don't go away. That's the gap long-term disability insurance is designed to cover.

You can get coverage through your employer, by shopping for an individual policy online, or through an insurance agent.

If your employer offers it, sign up. If not, get a private policy. If you rely on a paycheck, this coverage isn't optional.

LIFE INSURANCE

Life insurance isn't for you. It's for the people who need you when you're gone.

Its job is to replace your income so your family won't struggle, but the industry complicates it to sell you products you don't need.

The right choice is term-life insurance. It's straightforward and cheap. You pick the coverage amount and the length. If you die in that time, your family gets the payout.

Use the DIME method to figure out how much term life you need:

- **D - Debt:** Add up everything you owe today. You want all credit cards, student loans, car loans, etc. gone.
- **I - Income Replacement:** Start with 7 times your annual income so your family has time to adjust without rushing decisions. This covers everyday living costs and the help your household relied on, like childcare and house upkeep. More dependents or a single income usually means more coverage. Fewer dependents or a working spouse can mean less. Modestly rounding up is reasonable to account for inflation.
- **M - Mortgage Payoff:** How much is left on your mortgage? Add it.

- **E - Education:** Estimate the cost of college and childcare for your kids.

Add it all up. That's your term life amount.

Term lengths typically range from 5 to 30 years. The longer the term, the more expensive it gets. For most people, 20 years is a good fit. Rates are more affordable than a 30-year policy, and by the end of it your kids are likely out of the house.

Choose a term that lasts until your kids are independent or your spouse retires.

Avoid whole life, universal life, or variable life. These are sold as investments, but they're expensive, bloated with fees, and built to confuse you. Whole life can cost 10 to 20 times more than term for the same payout. They market it as a savings plan, but it's not. The returns are weak, the terms are vague, and the fine print is designed to benefit one person: the salesperson.

Don't rely only on the policy you get through your job. If you leave or get laid off, that coverage ends. You need your own policy, one that follows you no matter where you work.

HOMEOWNERS INSURANCE

One burst pipe is all it takes to turn a normal house into a six-figure problem if you're not insured correctly.

WHAT IT COVERS

Homeowners insurance has three jobs: to rebuild your house, replace your stuff, and protect you from lawsuits.

- **Dwelling:** Pays to repair or rebuild your home after damage from fire, wind, lightning, hail, or vandalism. The limit is based on reconstruction cost, not the market price your home could sell for. These are two very different numbers.
- Underinsuring here is one of the most common claim problems, and it's how people end up paying out of pocket after a total loss.
- **Other Structures:** Detached garages, fences, and sheds. Covered, but with a separate limit.
- **Personal Property:** Furniture, clothing, electronics, usually 50-70% of your dwelling limit. Jewelry, watches, and collectibles are capped unless you buy extra coverage.
- **Loss of Use:** Covers hotel stays, meals, or temporary housing if your home is unlivable after a covered claim.
- **Liability:** Protects you if someone sues after being hurt on your property. Pays for legal fees, medical bills, and judgments.
- **Medical Payments:** Covers small injuries to guests, from $1,000 to $10,000. Designed to settle minor problems before they worsen.

WHAT IT DOESN'T COVER

These common risks usually aren't included in a standard policy.

- Floods
- Earthquakes
- Sewer or drain backups
- Routine wear and tear
- Mold

If you need protection for these, ask your agent about separate policies or add-ons.

WHAT TO WATCH FOR

- **Deductible:** This is how much you pay before insurance kicks in. A higher deductible lowers your premium but means you pay more out of pocket when something goes wrong. Don't choose one you can't afford to pay.
- **Reconstruction cost:** Make sure the coverage amount is based on what it costs to rebuild, not what Zillow says your house is worth. Those are two different numbers.
- **Policy type:** Most homeowners policies are "HO-3," which is the standard policy most homeowners have and usually enough for typical risks.
- **Condo owners:** If you live in a condo, your needs are different. You don't insure the whole building, just your

unit's interior. Ask your insurance agent for an "HO-6" condo policy. The condo association covers the exterior. Always check your by-laws for specifics.

- **Wind and storm coverage:** Most policies cover hurricanes under "wind," but in some coastal or high-risk states that coverage can be excluded or written on a separate policy. Check with your agent to make sure you're covered.

- **Shopping your policy:** Insurance premiums change. Don't assume loyalty gets you the best deal. Shop your coverage every few years, or sooner if you see a major increase in price.

You're protecting the asset that everything else in your plan sits on. Get this wrong, and one bad claim can erase years of progress.

RENTERS INSURANCE

If you rent and would struggle to replace your belongings out of pocket, you need renters insurance.

It's cheap. Usually $10 to $20 a month. And it protects more than you think. More than half of renters have no insurance at all. That means one fire can leave you starting over.

WHAT IT COVERS

Renters insurance has three main parts:

- **Personal property:** Covers your belongings if they're damaged or stolen. That includes clothes, furniture, electronics, and more, even if they're taken from your car or lost during travel. Most policies cover common losses like fire, theft, and vandalism.
- **Liability:** Protects you if someone gets hurt at your place or if you accidentally cause damage to someone else's property. This includes legal costs if you're sued, which can add up fast.
- **Loss of use:** Pays for temporary housing and other living expenses if your apartment becomes unlivable after a covered event like fire or water damage.

WHAT IT DOESN'T COVER

Renters insurance doesn't cover the structure itself. That's your landlord's job. Some causes of loss aren't covered for your belongings, including:

- Flood damage (requires a separate flood policy)
- Pest infestations like bed bugs or rodents
- Your roommate's belongings, unless they're listed on your policy

Also, some valuables like jewelry or collectibles may be capped unless you buy extra coverage.

WHY IT MATTERS

Don't assume your landlord's policy protects you. It doesn't. If your apartment burns down, your clothes, laptop, and furniture are all gone. No reimbursement unless you have your own policy.

If a friend slips in your apartment and breaks an arm, renters insurance can cover their medical bills and protect you if they sue.

Most renters don't realize how exposed they are until a claim happens and there's no coverage to fall back on.

LONG-TERM CARE INSURANCE

The average nursing home costs about $100,000 per year. Assisted living can be almost as high. If you don't plan for that risk, your family will end up managing it for you, in time, money, or both.

About 70% of people over age 65 will need some form of long-term care, and the cost can wreck your plans if you're not ready.

Long-term care insurance isn't medical insurance. It doesn't cover doctor visits or hospital stays. It helps when you can no longer manage daily life on your own. That includes help with bathing, dressing, or conditions like Alzheimer's or Parkinson's. It covers in-home caregivers, assisted living, adult day care, and nursing homes.

Medicaid only steps in when you have spent down nearly all your assets, and the care options are limited. You may face long waitlists and little choice in where you end up.

Long-term care insurance helps protect against that, giving you more control over where you receive care and taking the pressure off your family. You might assume you can use retirement savings to pay for care yourself. The risk is needing care for years, or needing it earlier than expected while your spouse still needs support.

The average nursing home stay is just under 14 months, but 1 in 5 people will need care for five years or longer.

You don't need to buy this coverage while you're young. The best time to look is usually in your late 50s. At that point, premiums are still affordable and you avoid paying for decades before it's needed. If you wait too long, premiums may be out of reach or you risk not qualifying due to health reasons.

When shopping, look for inflation protection, which helps your benefits keep up with rising care costs. Get at least 3 to 5 years of coverage.

If you have savings, you can raise the elimination period, which is essentially a deductible measured in time. This is the number of days you pay before coverage starts. Stretching it from 30 to 90 days can cut premiums by 20% to 30%.

IDENTITY THEFT PROTECTION

Identity theft is one of the fastest-growing financial risks. It happens when someone uses your information to access your accounts or open new ones. They can open credit cards, take out loans, file false tax returns, or use your medical information to get treatment in your name. Fixing the mess can take months or years if you're unprepared.

About 1 in 3 Americans has dealt with some form of identity theft or fraud, often without realizing it until damage is done.

That's where identity theft protection helps. You can't stop every scam, so you need to make sure you're not alone when it happens. If someone hijacks your identity, you need more than an alert email. You want the cleanup handled for you and coverage that helps pay for the damage.

Look for these three essentials.

1. **Full restoration:** Professionals who dispute charges, work with credit bureaus, contact banks, and fix the mess for you. Monitoring alone isn't enough.
2. **$1 million in coverage:** To handle stolen funds, legal fees, and lost wages from cleanup.
3. **Monitoring:** Credit and dark web alerts, so you know early if your data is being used or sold.

Many people don't realize how exposed they are until accounts are frozen or credit applications start getting denied.

Common scams include phishing emails, fake IRS notices, and scammers filing tax returns in your name.

You don't need to spend much. Many good plans cost $10 to $20 a month. Some employers or banks include basic protection at no cost. Just don't assume your credit card company has you covered. They are protecting their money, not yours. This is about protecting your financial life.

TRAVEL INSURANCE

If you get sick or injured overseas, your health insurance at home may treat it as out-of-network care or may not cover you at all. Even if it does, foreign hospitals can still require full payment up front. There are no guarantees once you leave the country. Without travel insurance, you could be stuck with the entire bill.

Cruises are the biggest example. If something goes wrong at sea where you need emergency treatment, an airlift back to the United States can cost $50,000 to $100,000. Without coverage, you could be responsible for the full cost.

That's where travel insurance makes sense. A good policy covers emergency medical care and evacuation. Trip cancellation and delays are secondary benefits. It can also help if your luggage is lost, your flight is delayed, or your tour is canceled due to weather or illness.

If you're staying within the United States, you usually don't need it. Most care will be covered as normal. If you're leaving the country or stepping onto a cruise ship, medical-only travel insurance is worth the nominal fee.

WHAT TO SKIP

These types of insurance are often pushed hard, but they rarely protect real risks.

- Pet insurance. A sinking fund is a better option.
- Extended warranties on electronics and appliances. They're priced to favor the seller, not you.
- Mortgage life insurance. Use regular term life instead. Mortgage life is a fallback, not a strategy.
- Accidental death and dismemberment. If you already have term and disability coverage, this adds very little.
- Insurance sold as investments, like whole life or universal life. These are expensive, complex, and unnecessary for most households.

Skip products that protect convenience. Focus on coverage that protects income, housing, health, and liability. Everything else is noise.

Managing risk is what keeps you in the game. Protect what matters, skip what doesn't, and get back to building your life.

REMEMBER THIS

- Insurance protects wealth.
- Don't carry minimum auto limits.
- Disability insurance is paycheck protection.
- Buy term life. Skip the rest.
- Your home, your stuff, and your liability all need protection.
- Long-term care protects your retirement from the risk no one talks about.
- Protect what you've built.

CHAPTER 13

HSA: THE MOST OVERLOOKED WEALTH TOOL IN AMERICA

Most people treat an HSA like a gimmicky savings account. A place to park money for copays, prescriptions, and save a few dollars on taxes. As of 2024, Americans held nearly $147 billion in HSAs, but only 9% of accounts had any money invested.

An HSA isn't just for current medical expenses. It's also designed to hold pre-tax dollars that can grow over time and come out tax-free for qualified medical expenses later in life, including medically necessary long-term care.

When HSA money sits entirely in cash, the long-term advantage never compounds. The bigger value is having a healthcare buffer already in place when medical risk shows up, whether that's next year or decades from now.

HSA VS FSA: WHY IT'S NOT EVEN CLOSE

You can only contribute to an HSA if you're enrolled in a high-deductible health plan (HDHP). An HDHP without a funded HSA shifts more risk onto you, and without cash set aside, that risk can show up fast. Any money contributed to a HSA is permanently yours.

By contrast, Flexible Spending Accounts (FSAs) are offered alongside PPO (non-HDHP) plans. With an FSA, you spend it by year-end or lose it, and you can't invest the balance.

THE SMARTEST TAX BREAK YOU ARE SKIPPING

The tax savings are immediate and significant.

There is a reason financial professionals call this the tax trifecta. It's one of the only accounts that offers:

- Tax-deductible contributions
- Tax-free growth
- Tax-free withdrawals when used for qualified medical expenses

For 2026, you can contribute up to $4,400 as an individual or $8,750 as a family, plus an extra $1,000 each year once you hit 55.

If you max out $4,400 in the 22% bracket and include payroll taxes, you save about $1,320 in taxes that year. Skip the HSA and you pay those taxes without getting any medical buffer in return.

Over 30 years, that adds up to more than $132,000 contributed and about $39,000 saved in taxes. That's before factoring in investment growth or tax-free withdrawals.

THE YEAR OUR HSA PAID OFF BIG

I opened my HSA several years before my son was born. Back then, my medical costs were minimal, but I knew that wouldn't last. I kept contributing year after year, even though it didn't feel urgent.

Once we found out we were expecting, the expenses showed up fast. Labs, ultrasounds, extra appointments, and we weren't even halfway through the pregnancy. By the time our son was born in October, we had already hit our deductible, and the bills kept coming into the next year too.

The difference was that we were ready. The HSA meant we didn't have to debate care or scramble for cash. We stayed the extra night, did the follow-ups, and when the first year of daycare sickness and routine visits pushed us back to the deductible again, we handled it the same way.

YOUR HSA'S SECOND GEAR

Most providers let you invest once you pass the common $1,000 threshold.

The rule is simple. Keep at least your deductible in cash or a money market fund. If you want a larger safety net, hold up to your maximum out-of-pocket. Invest everything above that.

From there, the account stops being transactional and starts compounding.

I will get into investing strategy later in the book, but for now, know this: the HSA doesn't sit idle. It can grow alongside your other retirement accounts.

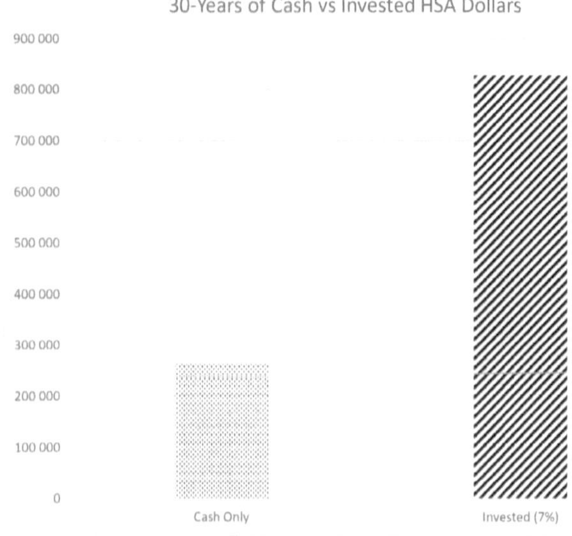

If you maxed out a family HSA for 30 years, it would grow to about $827,000 at a 7% return with steady contributions. Leave it in cash and you would have about $263,000. That single choice is worth about $564,000.

THE SHIELD AGAINST MEDICAL COSTS

There are two key reasons to keep building this fund. The first is choice. The last thing you want during a health scare is to choose care based on cost.

The second reason is retirement planning. According to Fidelity's 2024 Retiree Health Care Cost Estimate, the average 65-year-old can expect to spend about $165,000 on out-of-pocket health care costs throughout retirement. For a couple, that's $330,000.

This estimate assumes you are covered by Medicare Parts A, B, and D, which handle hospital care, doctor visits, and prescriptions, but Medicare doesn't cover everything. You still pay for dental and vision care, over-the-counter medications, Medicare premiums, and long-term care like nursing homes or in-home help. Your HSA can help cover those costs too.

Even if you start in your 50s, this account still matters, especially with catch-up contributions.

THE STRATEGY MOST PEOPLE MISS

Once you turn 65, your HSA becomes more versatile. You can use it for non-medical expenses just like a traditional IRA. You'll pay ordinary income tax on those withdrawals, but there's no penalty.

Unlike traditional retirement accounts, the HSA has no required minimum distributions. You can let the money sit and grow for as long as you want.

There's also no deadline to reimburse yourself for a qualified medical expense that happened after you opened your HSA. As long as you kept the receipt and didn't deduct the expense elsewhere, you can reimburse yourself whenever you want.

Let's say between ages 40 and 65, your family pays $2,400 per year out of pocket for qualified medical expenses. That's $60,000 over 25 years. If you save those receipts, you can reimburse yourself later, meaning you can withdraw that same amount from your HSA at any point, completely tax-free.

And while that money sits in your HSA, it grows. This approach is referred to as the "shoebox strategy."

This works for your children's expenses too, as long as they were dependents at the time of care.

By cash flowing your current medical expenses and delaying reimbursement, you create a future pool of tax-free cash that's ready when you need it.

WHY THE HSA BELONGS IN EVERY PLAN

If you have major healthcare needs and no savings cushion, an HDHP may not be the right fit today. But for most households, pairing an HDHP with a properly funded HSA shifts predictable medical risk into something you can plan for.

When you die, your spouse takes the account over and keeps using it.

If you qualify and ignore it, you're not being conservative. You're just leaving yourself exposed to one of the most predictable risks in life.

REMEMBER THIS

- An HSA is a retirement account with triple tax benefits.
- Keep at least your deductible in cash. Invest once your balance grows.
- Retirement health costs hit about $165,000 per person. Plan for it now.
- After 65, you can use your HSA like an IRA with no penalty.
- Join the 9% who invest.

CHAPTER 14

RETIREMENT: HOW TO WIN THE LONG GAME

Retirement doesn't get decided in a single moment. It takes shape in the earlier years that don't stand out.

When I took karate as a kid, my instructor used to say, "It's not who wants it the most the day of the fight. It's who wanted it most several months before." That line always stuck with me.

His example was simple. One fighter trains every day while the other sits on the couch eating pizza. On fight night, the one who skipped training acts shocked by the result. Retirement works the same way. The deposits are the training.

At the start, the stakes are easy to ignore. The balances are small, and the consequences feel far away. But the calendar keeps moving, and eventually the math stops being polite.

This chapter focuses on the few decisions that actually shape the outcome: how much to save, where to put it, and how to keep going when life changes and your attention drifts.

HOW MUCH TO SAVE

Estimating how much you'll need decades from now feels impossible. You're expected to guess your future expenses in a world that doesn't exist yet. Let's walk through an example so you can see what the numbers look like.

Henry is 35 and makes $100,000 a year. He plans to retire at 67, giving him 32 years to save. In his vision of retirement, the house is paid off, the kids are out of the house, and he's living comfortably. Fidelity states most retirees need about 70% to 80% of their income to maintain their lifestyle. That makes Henry's target of $75,000 a year reasonable.

Using the Federal Reserve's long-term inflation target of 2%, $75,000 today works out to roughly $141,000 when he retires.

Now the question is: how big of a nest egg does he need to safely pull $141,000 in his first year of retirement? Using the 4% rule, which is a guideline planners use to estimate safe withdrawals, that comes out to about $3.5 million.

The average 401k balance for people aged 35 to 44 is about $91,000. Let's use that as Henry's starting point. He gets a 4% employer match and a 2.5% raise each year. If he contributes 15% of his income, and his investments grow at 7% a year, he'll end up with just over $3.5 million by age 67.

Of that $3.5 million, about $718,000 came from Henry himself. His employer match totaled $193,000. The rest, just under $2.6 million, came from growth.

This is why saving 15% of your income (not counting the match) is a powerful long-term target. Some people will need more, especially if they start late or retire early.

So how do you decide how much to contribute without overthinking it?

THE RETIREMENT RAMP

The Retirement Ramp has three tiers that help you build momentum.

Here's how I break it down.

- **Tier 1: Match First**

   If your employer offers a match, get it. No debate. This is free money and the easiest return you'll ever get. Once you're past Step 2, make this your minimum contribution.

- **Tier 2: 15% - The Foundation**

   Once your housing is steady, this is the sweet spot. A consistent 15% of your income (not counting any employer match) stacks the odds in your favor.

- **Tier 3: 20% - Sleep-Easy Mode**

  If you want options, freedom, or just a bigger margin of safety, shoot for 20%. This tier gives you more flexibility for early retirement, market dips, or lifestyle changes down the road.

Use the ramp to keep making progress no matter what the economy is doing. The steeper the ramp, the sooner work becomes optional.

TYPES OF ACCOUNTS

TRADITIONAL VS ROTH

Most retirement accounts come in two flavors, Traditional and Roth. Both accounts help your money grow. The difference is when you pay the taxes. With a Traditional account, you get the tax break now. Your contributions reduce your taxable income today, but every dollar you pull out in retirement is taxed as income. With a Roth, it's the opposite. You pay taxes upfront, but your withdrawals are completely tax-free.

Most people are better off with Roth. There's no worrying about future tax rates, and the money grows and comes out tax-free for life. That kind of certainty is tough to beat. Traditional accounts can still make sense if you're in a high tax bracket or close enough to retirement to reasonably predict your taxes. Tax laws change, but the advantage of known taxes now usually beats guessing future rates.

401K

This is where most people build the bulk of their retirement savings. The 401k is offered by employers, and the key feature is the match. When a company matches what you put in, it's free money. The 2026 limit is $24,500. If you're 50 or older, you can add $8,000. Those ages 60 to 63 can add another $3,250. Withdrawals before age 59½ usually come with a 10% penalty unless an exception applies. Once you hit 73, required minimum distributions (RMDs) begin.

When you change jobs, you have a few choices. You can leave the account where it is, roll it into your new plan, or move it to an IRA. If your Roth 401k has weak investment choices, moving that portion into a Roth IRA can make sense. However, I recommend keeping the Traditional portion in a 401k so you don't close the door on a backdoor Roth, since those rules look at all your IRA balances together. For most people, the cleanest option is to just roll everything into your new 401k and keep it all in one place.

INDIVIDUAL RETIREMENT ACCOUNTS (IRAS)

IRAs exist to give you control when your workplace plan falls short or runs out of room. In 2026, you can contribute up to $7,500. If you're 50 or older, you can add another $1,100. A Traditional IRA may be tax deductible depending on your income and whether your job offers a plan. A Roth IRA works differently. It has strict income limits, and you can only contribute if you fall under those limits. Traditional IRAs also require you to start taking distributions at age 73. Roth IRAs don't have this rule.

Pulling money out early usually triggers penalties. Roth IRAs let you withdraw contributions anytime, but early withdrawals of gains still get taxed and penalized.

THE BACKDOOR ROTH IRA

The backdoor Roth IRA is a legal workaround that helps people who earn too much for a normal Roth to still get money into one.

Step one: Put money into a Traditional IRA.

Step two: Immediately convert it to a Roth IRA. If the money has already been taxed and you follow the rules, the conversion isn't taxed.

The tricky part is the IRS pro rata rule. If you keep any pretax money in a Traditional IRA, your Roth conversion will be partly taxable. The IRS treats all your IRA money as one big pot. It mixes your pretax and after-tax dollars together. You can't just convert the clean part by itself. That's why many people keep their pretax 401k money in a 401k. This keeps their Traditional IRA balance at zero when they do a backdoor Roth, so the conversion stays as clean and tax-efficient as possible.

403B AND 457B

Teachers, healthcare workers, and many nonprofit employees often get a 403b or 457b instead of a 401k. A 403b is the nonprofit version of a 401k. A 457b has one standout perk. If you leave your job, you can access the money without the 10% early withdrawal penalty.

In 2026, you can contribute $24,500, plus an $8,000 catch-up if you are 50 or older. If you have both a 403b and a 457b, you can contribute to each. Someone between 60 and 63 can save up to $68,250 by using the super catch-up in the 403b along with the regular catch-up in the 457b. One catch with 403b plans is that many of them use annuities with high fees and limited investment choices, so your money grows slower. Always read the fine print before you sign up.

OPTIONS FOR THE SELF-EMPLOYED

No one hands you a plan when you work for yourself, but you also have some of the most powerful tools available. These are the plans that let freelancers outsave Fortune 500 workers.

- **Solo 401k:** Lets you contribute as both employee and employer. In 2026, the combined limit is $69,000. You can contribute $24,500 as the employee and up to 25% of your business income as the employer. Add $8,000 if you are 50 or older. You can choose Roth or Traditional. Once your balance passes $250,000, you must file IRS

Form 5500-EZ annually. It's a short form that reports your account size to the IRS.

- **SEP IRA:** Easier to set up. Only the employer contributes, up to 25% of income, capped at the same $69,000 limit as the Solo 401k. There is no Roth option, and if you have employees, you must contribute equally for them.

- **SIMPLE IRA:** Built for businesses with fewer than 100 employees. In 2026, employees can contribute $17,000 and employers can match up to 3%. Add $4,000 if you are 50 or older. The catch is that withdrawals in the first two years face a steep 25% penalty.

INVESTMENT OPTIONS

Most retirement accounts give you choices for how your money is invested. That's great, but it also overwhelms a lot of people. The good news is you don't need to be an expert.

The simplest option is a Target Date Fund. These are designed to adjust automatically as you age and take on less risk as you get closer to retirement. They aren't perfect, but they're easy and keep the plan moving.

If someone had put $10,000 into a Target Date 2050 fund 10 years ago, it'd be worth over $20,000 today based on historical returns.

Some employers also offer managed accounts. That means someone picks and adjusts your investments for you. This can be helpful, but look at the fees. High fees drag down growth over time.

At this stage, consistency matters more than optimization. Don't wait for the perfect fund. Just keep contributing and give your money time to grow.

The next chapter builds on this foundation and shows how growth compounds over time once the system is in place.

ARE YOU ON TRACK?

Most people have no idea if they're on pace. Fidelity's retirement benchmarks offer simple checkpoints you can use as a quick gut check:

- Age 30: 1x your salary
- Age 35: 2x your salary
- Age 40: 3x your salary
- Age 45: 4x your salary
- Age 50: 6x your salary
- Age 55: 7x your salary
- Age 60: 8x your salary
- Age 67: 10x your salary

For example, if you're 40 and make $80,000, the checkpoint says you should have about $240,000 saved.

These numbers aren't requirements. They're mile markers, and fast income growth can make the targets look off. Your lifestyle, when you retire, and your health will always matter more than any chart.

WHAT IF YOU'RE BEHIND?

If you read that list and thought, "I'm nowhere close," don't panic. Falling short doesn't disqualify you. It just means the best time to start is right now.

Bump your contributions by 1% this year. Do it again next year. Those small increases are what keep time working for you instead of against you.

Treat each increase like one more step forward. Small moves stack fast.

SOCIAL SECURITY AND MEDICARE

Social Security provides monthly income, but it only replaces about 40% of your pre-retirement earnings. I like to think of it as a bonus, not a plan.

If Social Security is essential for your retirement to work, you're already relying on a fragile plan.

The average Social Security check is about $1,900 a month. The average retiree household spends more than $4,500 a month. It was never designed to carry the full load. That gap has to be filled by your own savings.

Medicare covers hospital and doctor visits starting at age 65, but it doesn't cover everything. Dental, vision, and long-term care are major gaps that catch people off guard. You still pay premiums and out-of-pocket costs.

A strong retirement plan makes these programs helpful, not necessary.

THE STAGES OF RETIREMENT

Planners often describe retirement in phases. Each one changes how you spend and plan.

PRE-RETIREMENT: GETTING READY

This is when retirement starts to feel real. You're still working, likely earning the most you ever have, but your mindset begins to shift. Retirement stops feeling distant and becomes a date on the calendar. It's also when that sense of being behind starts to feel more urgent.

EARLY RETIREMENT: THE GO-GO YEARS

You're finally done working and ready to enjoy it. Travel, hobbies, and new routines fill your calendar. These are the "go-go" years because spending often increases as you make the most of your freedom. You're active and engaged.

MID-RETIREMENT: THE SLOW-GO YEARS

As you reach your mid-70s, your energy drops and long trips don't sound as much fun. Life moves at a slower pace. This is often when health costs begin to rise.

LATE RETIREMENT: THE NO-GO YEARS

Eventually, most people reach a stage where independence becomes harder. The focus shifts to safety, comfort, and care. By the No-Go years, nearly 70% of retirees will need some form of long-term care, and most underestimate the costs. That's why long-term care planning matters, for you and for the people who love you.

A TALE OF TWO RETIREMENTS

Dale and John worked the same job and had the same opportunities, but they were two lives and retirements that couldn't look more different.

Dale lived with purpose. He wasn't reckless. He took his family on trips, ate at great restaurants, and enjoyed life, but he didn't throw money at things that didn't matter. He drove his cars for more than 10 years and drove one past 200,000 miles. He stayed in a house that fit his needs, and steadily invested throughout his career. He maxed out his retirement, funded his HSA, and picked up long-term care insurance in his late 50s.

Now, at 62, Dale is retired. His investments bring in more money every year than he ever earned on the job. He has no debt, no stress, and no reason to watch the stock market like a hawk. He still travels. Still spoils his grandkids. But the best part? He gets to do it on his terms.

John made the same money, but every raise turned into a new expense. He leased luxury cars and took expensive trips. He enjoyed one-upping people. He built a lifestyle he couldn't sustain. Retirement felt far off.

Then 65 arrived. On a ski trip with friends, John took a rough fall. His back never fully recovered, and climbing ladders for inspections was no longer in the cards. He wasn't ready to stop working, but he didn't have a choice.

He never saved beyond the company match. No cushion. No plan. He sold the house and moved into a condo. The car lease went away. Travel wasn't just off the table, it was gone from the conversation.

John could still walk. He just couldn't afford to go anywhere.

Dale has options.

John has constraints.

Those outcomes were driven by what happened while the money was working. The next chapter shifts from accounts and planning to how growth actually gets built over time. This is where discipline turns into compounding and where the gap between Dale and John widens every year.

REMEMBER THIS

- Climb the Retirement Ramp. Get the match, move to 15%, and push to 20% if you want options and flexibility.
- Compounding does the heavy lifting. Your job is to keep contributing.
- Social Security and Medicare help you, but they won't carry you.
- Plan for the stages of retirement so long-term care never blindsides you.
- It's never too late to start. Momentum beats perfection every time.

STEP 5:

QUIET WEALTH

This is the step that locks everything in.

Up to now, the work was about control. You stopped the bleeding and gave your money structure. You decided where it goes and what it protects, so progress never depends on luck or timing.

If money isn't invested, inflation slowly eats it. That's how people fall behind without noticing.

You earn more, but the extra gets absorbed. Markets feel confusing, so investing is put back. One year turns into a few. Compounding never gets the runway it needs.

You'll learn how markets actually behave over time and where most investors get themselves into trouble. Once you understand that, doing nothing no longer feels safer than staying invested.

It also changes how you act.

Watching the way other people spend can put you off your own plan. Comparison breaks consistency. Confidence comes from knowing what you're doing and sticking to it, not from keeping up with someone else's highlight reel.

Over time, investing does what effort can't. Your money grows faster than your costs and the gap widens in your favor.

Step 5 is about staying with the system long enough for that to happen.

CHAPTER 15

INVESTING – START SMALL, GROW BIG

One morning, I was driving my son to get his haircut before a trip to visit his great-grandparents and the song *"Tubthumping"* by Chumbawamba came on the radio. You know the one: "I get knocked down, but I get up again."

That's the stock market in one line.

Since 1928, there have been 27 bear markets where stocks fell at least 20%. The average drop was 35%, and the average recovery back to the prior high took about 2.5 years. Every single time, it came back.

That's why the market works. The problem is that most investors don't act like it will get back when it matters.

Instead of riding it out, they panic. They buy high, sell low, and chase hype. The S&P 500 has returned about 10% per year since 1928. The average investor earned materially less.

That gap isn't caused by bad markets.

It's caused by behavior breaking under pressure.

This chapter isn't about beating the market.

It's about building an investing system you don't abandon when things get uncomfortable.

WHAT IS "THE MARKET"?

When people say "the market," they're usually talking about the stock market as a whole, often the S&P 500, but investing is bigger than that. There are five major asset classes you need to know: cash, stocks, bonds, real estate, and alternatives.

Each one behaves differently and plays a different role. Once you understand what each one does, you can build a portfolio that fits your goals.

Before you jump into investing, you need to know the landscape. Here's what each one actually does.

CASH

Cash is safe, but it loses value over time. It's low risk but low reward.

A savings account might pay you 3% to 4% right now, but inflation eats that up. Over time, inflation has averaged about 3%. That means your money slowly buys less unless it grows faster than that.

Cash is what you use for short-term goals and your emergency fund, but it isn't a good place to build wealth.

STOCKS

Stocks are shares of companies. When you buy stock, you're buying ownership in that business. Stocks offer the best long-term returns of any asset class, but they're unpredictable in the short term. In 2020, they fell over 30% in a single month. That's the trade-off. Avoiding that volatility is how people miss the growth entirely. When you sit out, you usually miss the rebound that drives the best years.

Stocks are the growth engine of your portfolio.

BONDS

Bonds are loans. When you buy a bond, you're lending money to a company or the government in exchange for interest.

Bonds exist for stability. They don't swing like stocks do. They help smooth out the ride when markets get rough.

Nobody's popping champagne over bond returns. That's not their job. Bonds are there to keep a bad year from turning into a bad decade.

Bond funds let you hold many bonds at once, just like an index fund gives you exposure to many stocks.

REAL ESTATE

Real estate builds wealth in two ways: price growth and rental income. Both rise and fall because real estate has its own version of market swings.

You can own physical property, like a rental house, or you can invest in a REIT, a real estate investment trust. A REIT is a company that owns income-producing real estate, and you can buy shares the same way you buy a stock.

REITs have returned around 8% to 10% per year over the long run, but they come with risk, just like stocks. When interest rates rise or the economy slows, real estate values can drop. In 2008, prices fell over 20% and took years to recover.

A lot of people have gotten rich through physical real estate, but most of them took on a lot of debt to do so. If you want real estate without the hassle, REITs are the easier play.

ALTERNATIVES

This is the category most people lose money in.

Alternatives include crypto, commodities, gold, hedge funds, private equity, and anything else that doesn't fall into the other categories.

Let's take crypto. Bitcoin rose from under a dollar and went to the moon, then it fell more than 50%. Could it keep rising? Sure. Could it collapse again? Also, yes.

Most of the big names pushing alternatives are the ones making money off them. This is where chasing upside wrecks discipline.

If you want to add a small percentage once your core portfolio is in place, fine. Just don't start here. Don't chase what you don't understand.

PUTTING IT ALL TOGETHER

Every asset class has a role. Cash is for safety. Bonds are for stability. Stocks are for growth. Real estate adds income and diversification. For most people, alternatives are mostly noise. Think of these as risk buckets. Each behaves differently. Diversification protects you so one bad bucket can't wreck your plan.

You don't need every asset class to build wealth. You just need to know what each piece does, what it's good for, and what it's not.

The rest of this chapter will focus on stocks: how to understand them, how to invest in them, and how to stay the course when everyone is screaming to bail.

This is where the real growth happens.

INDEX AND MUTUAL FUNDS

When you invest in a fund, you're buying a basket of companies in one shot, but not all baskets are built the same.

INDEX FUNDS

An index fund is a group of stocks that follows a preset list. That list is called an index. Index funds can be bought as either an exchange traded fund (ETF) or a mutual fund. An ETF trades throughout the day like a stock, while a mutual fund trades once per day after the market closes.

One of the most popular indexes is the S&P 500, which includes 500 of the largest companies in the U.S. When you buy an S&P 500 index fund, you own a small slice of every company on that list. You don't have to pick stocks yourself. The fund does that for you by copying the index. This is called passive investing.

Most index funds are weighted by size. That means you'll own more of big companies like Apple and Microsoft than you will of Ford or Delta Air Lines. It's based on market cap, not equal slices for every company.

Companies can show up in more than one index. A company could be in the S&P 500, a growth index, and a tech index.

There are two main reasons index funds work so well: cost and performance. They're cheap to own and hard to beat. A simple starting point for many investors is the S&P 500 index fund. It's low cost and has a long track record of strong returns.

You're not trying to outsmart the market. You're just riding with it. Investing isn't supposed to be flashy. If it feels simple, you're doing it right.

ACTIVELY MANAGED MUTUAL FUNDS

These funds aim to beat the market. A professional fund manager researches companies, looks at economic trends, and decides which stocks to buy and sell. Some funds lean heavily into certain industries. Others make bold bets based on what they think will happen next.

An example of this would be an S&P 500 actively managed mutual fund. Instead of the index, which holds all stocks in the index, a fund manager may buy more of a company currently doing well or reduce holdings that are underperforming.

Sometimes it works, but most of the time it doesn't. Even if they pick the right stocks, higher fees can wipe out the gains. And many managers don't beat the index at all.

You also won't always know what the fund owns unless you dig into the full list of holdings. That's one more layer of complexity you don't need.

If you're investing through a 401k or similar plan, you may only have access to actively managed mutual funds. That's fine. What matters is how much you save and how long you stay invested.

WHY INDEX FUNDS WIN

Let's talk fees.

Vanguard's S&P 500 index fund (VOO) charges a fee of 0.03%. That's 30 cents per $1,000 invested every year. Compare that to a typical actively managed mutual fund, which might charge 1% or more, especially if you're investing through an advisor. That's $10 per $1,000, over 30 times higher. The gap is what fees take from you.

Fees matter more than most people think. If you invest $100,000 and let it grow at 8% for 30 years, here's what happens:

The index fund grows to about $998,000. The mutual fund with a 1% fee grows to about $761,000.

That gap is the cost of fees over time. Even a single percent can erase hundreds of thousands of dollars over a career.

And that's before investor behavior gets in the way. Many retail investors, people who buy and sell for their own account, buy high and sell low. They panic and chase hype. That's how people lose. Index funds help prevent that. You set it and leave it alone.

John Bogle, the founder of Vanguard, built his life's work around this idea. He famously said only 1 in 14 actively managed mutual funds beats the market over time. Those aren't odds you bet on.

A REAL EXAMPLE OF FEES IN ACTION

If you put $10,000 into the Fidelity 500 Index Fund (FXAIX) in 2016, you would have paid almost nothing in fees with its 0.015% expense ratio. By the end of 2025, that money grew to about $39,000.

If instead you put the same $10,000 into American Funds Washington Mutual (AWSHX), with its 0.59% expense ratio and 5.75% front load fee, you would have ended up with about $33,000.

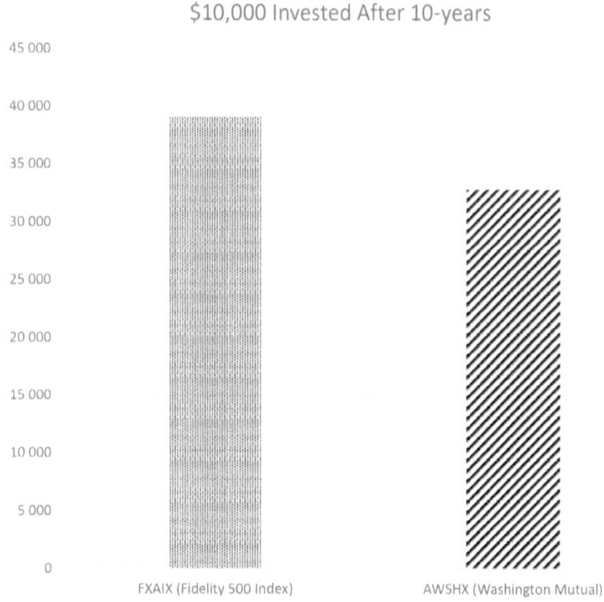

That's a $6,000 gap, with nearly $4,000 coming from fees and upfront commission.

A QUICK NOTE ON TAXES

Retirement accounts like a 401k or IRA don't get taxed each year as they grow. You only pay taxes when you take the money out in retirement.

The exception is a Roth. With a Roth, you pay taxes up front. That means the money you put in already has already had taxes taken out from your paycheck. Once it's in the Roth, it grows tax-free, and you don't pay taxes when you take it out later.

Taxable accounts work differently. You can invest in the same funds, but you pay taxes as you go. If the fund pays dividends, you owe taxes that same year. If you sell and make a gain, you owe taxes on that gain.

THE BOTTOM LINE

Index funds keep it simple. They're low cost, transparent, and time-tested.

Actively managed funds are a mixed bag. Some are decent. Many are overpriced. Only a few ever beat the index.

If you want the odds in your favor, the data is clear on this. Low-cost index funds give you a better shot at long-term success than trying to beat the market. Your job is to stay invested and keep costs low. Everything else is noise.

FINANCIAL ADVISORS

You don't need a financial advisor to build wealth, but some people still want one. If you're going to pay someone to help manage your money, you need to understand what they do and how much it'll cost you.

BRUCE'S STORY

Financial advisors can be helpful. A good advisor can keep costs low, help you stay on track, and stop you from making emotional decisions when the market takes a hit.

But here's the truth: many financial advisors are trained in sales first, and finance second.

I have a friend named Bruce who opened a traditional IRA because his advisor told him it would help with taxes. Bruce set it up then ignored it. One day I asked him how it was invested. He wasn't sure, but he trusted me enough to show me the statement.

It was just a basic S&P 500 index fund.

Nothing special, but Bruce was paying a 1.5% fee every year.

That's a high price to pay for something he could've done himself. However, Bruce doesn't want to manage it. He likes having someone to call if he needs help.

And that's the point. Personal finance is personal.

If you want help and accept the cost, that's your call. Just make sure your advisor works for you, not the commission.

HOW ADVISOR FEES WORK

Most financial advisors charge based on how much money you have invested with them. It's called an AUM fee, short for assets under management. The standard fee is around 1% to 2% per year.

It doesn't sound like much, but over 30 years, even a 1% fee can add up.

If you have a $1M portfolio, that's $10k per year in fees whether you make money or not.

Other advisors work on commission. They get paid when they sell you certain products, like insurance plans, annuities, or expensive mutual funds. This is where a lot of people get burned. You walk in thinking you're getting advice. You walk out with a high-fee product that makes them money, not you.

The third type is fee-only. These advisors charge a flat rate or an hourly fee, and they don't get paid based on what you buy. They're less common, but they exist. If you're going to hire someone, this is the setup to look for.

The wrong advisor can take more from you in fees than they ever give back in value. And you don't get that risk back.

DO YOU EVEN NEED A FINANCIAL ADVISOR?

Most people don't. If you grasp the basics of index funds, diversification, and the basic tax rules, you're fine without one. You can automate everything and still come out ahead of most investors who use a "pro."

But if you own a business, are dealing with a big inheritance, or just don't feel comfortable on your own, a good advisor can help.

Just don't assume that expensive equals smart. Or that all advisors are fiduciaries, meaning they're legally required to act in your best interest.

THREE QUESTIONS TO ASK

If you decide to work with an advisor, ask these three questions up front:

1. How do you get paid?
2. Do you receive commissions on products you recommend?
3. Are you a fiduciary?

If they dodge or downplay those questions, walk. As mentioned, most advisors aren't fiduciaries, but that doesn't automatically make them bad. The important thing is that they act in your best interest.

You don't owe anyone blind trust just because they wear a suit and talk fast.

THE BOTTOM LINE

The financial world is full of people who sound smart and charge a lot to do what you could do yourself with a low-cost index fund.

If you want the service, that's fine. Just know what you're paying for and what you're getting in return.

And remember: nobody will ever care more about your money than you do. Don't hand over control just because it feels easier in the moment.

BREAKING DOWN STOCK TYPES

Not all stocks are built the same. They're grouped by size, style, and geography. These categories aren't just labels. They affect risk, returns, and how your portfolio reacts when the market moves.

We're going a little deeper now. Stick with me and you'll see why this matters and how simple it really is.

BY SIZE

Stock size is based on market cap, short for market capitalization. Market cap sounds like fancy finance talk, but it's just the stock market's way of saying how much a company is worth: stock price times the total number of shares outstanding.

Size comes with different levels of risk. Bigger companies move more slowly. Smaller ones have bigger swings.

Large-cap stocks are the big dogs. These are companies like Apple, Microsoft, and Amazon. They're well known, established, and steadier than smaller companies. Most index funds lean heavy on large-caps, and for good reason. They make up the bulk of the market and usually pay dividends.

Mid-cap stocks are companies like Crocs and Harley-Davidson. They aren't massive, but they aren't startups either. These companies still have room to grow, but they're past the "prove-it" stage. They tend to bounce around more than large-caps, but that's part of the trade-off. More upside also means more noise.

Then you have small-cap stocks. These are smaller companies with more price swings and a wider range of outcomes. A good example is Denny's. Some small-caps grow fast. Some stay flat for years. Some never make it. When the economy is strong, small-caps often rise faster. When things slow down, they usually drop harder. More upside also means more volatility.

If you had bought Amazon back in 1997 when it was a small-cap, a $1,000 investment would be worth over $3 million in 2026. But most small-caps don't turn into Amazon. That's why diversification matters. You're not trying to find the golden ticket. You're just buying the whole chocolate factory.

BY STYLE

Stocks also get grouped into value and growth.

Value stocks are usually mature and more stable companies that trade at a discount compared to their earnings or assets. They often pay dividends and don't grow fast, but they hold up better when the market drops. Think companies like Clorox or Coca-Cola. Boring, but in a good way.

Growth stocks are companies expected to grow fast. They usually don't pay dividends because they reinvest all their profits to keep growing. That can mean big gains, but it also means bigger drops when things go wrong. Think Tesla, Nvidia, or Shopify.

Neither style wins forever. Growth might dominate for a few years, then value comes roaring back. Most index funds include both, so you don't have to pick a side.

BY GEOGRAPHY

Most U.S. investors stick to U.S. stocks, and for good reason. The U.S. market has crushed most others over the last couple of decades, but there are still reasons to look outside the country.

International stocks are usually split into developed and emerging markets.

Developed markets include countries like Germany, Japan, and the United Kingdom. These economies are stable, the legal systems are strong, and the companies are mature. Returns tend to be lower, but so is the risk. Emerging markets are faster growing but more unpredictable. That unpredictability is the trade-off for higher potential returns. Think countries like India, Brazil, or China. Political issues, currency problems, and weaker legal systems all add risk, but if things go well, the upside is higher.

From 2003 to 2007, emerging markets outperformed the U.S. by a wide margin. Since then, U.S. stocks have dominated. It swings back and forth. That's the case for holding a small slice of international stocks. You're spreading your risk across different countries instead of betting everything on one.

A lot of investors aim for 10% to 40% of their stock portfolio in international funds. You don't need to overthink it. Some skip it entirely. I stick to the 20% range. Enough to get the benefits without adding unnecessary complexity.

KNOW WHAT YOU OWN

This is about giving you control and knowing what's in your portfolio. When you see a fund that says "small-cap value" or "international growth," you'll know exactly what that means.

AVERAGE HISTORICAL PERFORMANCE

Before you start investing, you need to know what you're signing up for. You're signing up for growth with swings.

Let's look at how the market has actually performed over time. The ups, the crashes, the recoveries, and everything in between.

STOCKS OVER TIME

If you had invested $1,000 in the S&P 500 at the start of 1975 and reinvested all the dividends, that investment would be worth about $268k by the end of 2024. That's an average return of about 11.8% per year.

Now let's adjust for inflation, because that's what really matters. Your real return would be closer to 8% per year. The long-term reward is the payoff for staying through the swings.

This pattern shows up in every long stretch of time. Over the last 100 years, U.S. stocks have returned between 9% and 10% per year on average. Some decades are better. Some are brutal.

But the long-term trend has been steady growth, as long as you stay invested.

S&P 500 Price, 1928-2024: This is what "staying invested" really looks like.

I've seen this play out in my own 401k. For the first few years, it didn't feel like anything was happening, but around year eight, I started to notice that the growth picked up. The snowball started rolling.

I've also experienced a few panic moments. The COVID crash was nail-biting, and the 10-month bear market in 2022 dragged on forever. Every crash feels different, but the patterns are the same. It would've been easy to bail, but I didn't. I stuck with the plan.

WHAT ABOUT BONDS AND GOLD?

Bonds are steady but slow. They're there for stability. Over the past 50 years, the average return for all types of bonds was about 5% per year.

Gold is often pitched as a hedge against inflation, but the truth is gold's long-term return barely keeps up with inflation at all. From 1975 to 2024, gold returned about 2% per year after inflation. That's worse than stocks, bonds, and real estate.

WHAT THIS REALLY MEANS

Stocks win over time, but they don't go up in a straight line.

You'll see crashes. You'll doubt the process. The people who jump out lose. The people who stay in get rewarded.

7% per year might not sound exciting, but it doubles your money roughly every 10 years. And the earlier you start, the less you have to save to reach your goal.

You don't need perfect timing or a magic fund. You need discipline when the market moves.

BEHAVIOR AND MINDSET

If I asked you to name one trait that shows up in the best-performing accounts at Fidelity, you'd probably guess they're owned by economists, CEOs, or people who work on Wall Street.

But the actual answer? Dead people. And people who forgot they had an account.

That's the story, anyway. It's become a popular line in the investing world. Turns out it's nothing more than an urban legend, but the lesson behind it carries a lot of truth.

Real studies have shown people tend to buy high, usually after the market's been doing great, and then panic and sell low when things get rough. The exact opposite of what works. They don't mean to do this. It's just human nature.

You need a long-term mindset. If you'll need the money within five years, think about whether investing makes sense.

The market is like the weather. It's messy in the short term and wild day to day, but the long-term pattern is steady. Seasons always change. One day of rain doesn't ruin the season. One bad year doesn't ruin your future.

A study from Dalbar showed that over a 30-year period, the average investor earned 3% to 5% less per year than the market. The gap came from bad timing and emotional decisions. They bought after big runs, sold after big drops, and missed the recoveries.

The biggest risk in investing isn't the market. It's what you do when the market moves.

THE SIMPLE FORMULA

WLADIMIR KLITSCHKO: WINNING WITH THE BASICS

Wladimir Klitschko was a heavyweight boxer who won the Olympic gold in 1996 at age 20 and later became a world champion.

He wasn't a flashy fighter. His whole approach was fundamentals and control. Jab. Right cross. Control distance. Reset. Over and over. He was frequently criticized for being boring, but it worked.

Early in his pro career, he took brutal knockout losses and got labeled "chinny." Instead of chasing flash, he rebuilt around discipline. Under trainer Emanuel Steward, he doubled down on the basics and became one of the most dominant heavyweights of his era.

He didn't win by being spectacular. He won by being consistent.

THE INVESTING PUNCHLINE

Klitschko's story lines up with investing in a way most people miss. The things that actually work rarely make headlines. You don't see news stories about people quietly becoming millionaires by investing in broad index funds and sticking with them for decades, even though that's how it happens for a lot of people.

Every now and then, someone really does catch lightning in a bottle. Maybe they bought Bitcoin in 2013. Maybe they bought Apple in the 90s. Knowing about something early isn't the same as having the discipline to stick with it, and it isn't the same as having a repeatable plan.

That's where people get pulled off course. It's easy to look back and think, "I should've done that," or convince yourself you can catch the next big run, but that isn't investing. That's chasing outcomes after the fact.

The market rewards steady behavior. Investing in something broad and low-cost, contributing consistently, and then leaving it alone. The people who do that don't make for interesting stories, but they're the ones who end up winning in the long run.

The formula isn't exciting. It's the same one Klitschko relied on.

Low-cost, broad market index funds. Time in the market. Compounding does the rest.

REMEMBER THIS

- Every crash in history has recovered.
- Fees kill wealth. Even 1% can drain hundreds of thousands.
- Low-cost broad market index funds are the best bet most investors will ever have.
- Diversification keeps one crash from sinking you.
- Staying calm and invested beats being clever.
- Time, not timing, builds wealth.
- Most people don't lose to the market. They lose to themselves.

CHAPTER 16

STOP COUNTING OTHER PEOPLE'S MONEY

We live in a world built to make you compare. Your neighbor buys a luxury car. Your coworker flies to Italy. The message is subtle, but constant. You're behind. That comparison doesn't motivate you. It distorts you.

You start making money decisions based on what other people appear to be doing instead of what actually works. You stretch a little more. You upgrade a little faster. You justify things you wouldn't have touched if no one was watching.

The problem is that you're comparing yourself to a highlight reel. You don't see the trade-offs behind the scenes. And when you set your standards off someone else's snapshot, progress slows or stops entirely.

Most people never realize how much money leaks away trying to match everyone around them. Quiet money compounds. Loud money leaks.

The sooner you stop counting other people's money, the faster you can build your own.

JORDAN. LEBRON. MAGIC. BRIDGEMAN?

What do these four NBA players have in common? They're the only ones who built fortunes that surpassed $1 billion (*The Wall Street Journal, 2025*).

Everyone knows the first three. Jordan is the GOAT. LeBron is legendary. Magic was transformative.

So, who's the fourth?

Junior Bridgeman.

In 1975, the Lakers drafted Bridgeman eighth overall, then traded him to Milwaukee before he ever played a game. That deal sent Kareem Abdul-Jabbar to Los Angeles. Bridgeman played 12 years in the league. He was a reliable sixth man. Coaches trusted him.

His highest salary was about $350,000 for a season. That's a strong income, but not enough to carry you for life with a career that often ends by your early thirties. He could have spent it trying to keep pace with the stars of his era. Instead, he paid attention. He studied business, read contracts, and learned how companies made money.

He bought a few Wendy's franchises and worked the drive-thru to learn the operation from the ground up. Over time, those restaurants grew into hundreds. He added Chili's and Fazoli's, then moved into Coca-Cola bottling and other businesses. By the mid-2010s, Bridgeman had quietly built one of the largest franchise and bottling operations in the country.

At the time of his death in 2025, his fortune was reported at around $1.4 billion, placing him just behind Michael Jordan among NBA players in wealth.

Bridgeman didn't win the spotlight. He won the long game.

STOP SPENDING EVERY RAISE

When Shaq signed his first NBA contract in 1992, he walked out with a million-dollar check. Within 30 minutes, it was spoken for. A Mercedes for himself. Another for his dad. One for his mom. The money was gone before he ever played a game.

A banker friend pulled him aside and warned him he was on track to go broke if he kept burning through money. He didn't want to hear it, but he listened. Then he changed.

Shaq earned more than $290 million during his NBA career, but he built more after he retired. He made more after basketball because he stopped trying to outspend everyone else. He started building businesses and made investments that kept paying.

He summed it up simply: "It's not about how much you make; it's about how much you keep."

That's lifestyle creep. Spending rises with income until the raise disappears and nothing really changes.

It rarely feels reckless. A meal kit. A new streaming service. Lawn care. House cleaning. $50 here. $100 there. By the end of the month, the entire raise is gone, and the stress level hasn't moved.

When your income goes up, lock part of it away before you upgrade anything. Make it automatic. A simple rule is to save or invest at least half of every raise.

Look at two coworkers, Nate and Tony, both close in age and earning about the same. On the surface, their lives looked worlds apart. Tony lived loud. Nate didn't.

Tony bought the biggest house he could get approved for. He leased luxury cars and dressed sharp. Nate's house was nice, but not oversized. His cars were paid off and in great shape. He still had fun. He was a season ticket holder for his favorite team, but the tickets were saved for and paid in full. His splurges were planned, not constant.

They both had two kids around the same age. One day in the breakroom, Tony was stressing about college costs and Parent PLUS loans. Nate walked in, and someone asked if his oldest had picked a school. Nate said yes. Scholarships? "Nope. I've got the first five years covered. After that, they're on their own."

Tony looked rich. Nate had margin.

THREE SIMPLE RULES TO BEAT LIFESTYLE CREEP

1. Freeze your lifestyle for 6 to 12 months after a raise.
2. Review your recurring bills every year.
3. Save at least half of every raise.

These rules keep your money from leaking out the back while you're trying to move forward.

CARS, WATCHES, AND THE ILLUSION OF WEALTH

Movies and social media tell us millionaires live in oversized houses, drive luxury cars, and collect expensive watches.

Research, including *The Millionaire Next Door*, shows most wealthy households don't drive high-end brands. The most common cars among millionaires have long been Fords, Toyotas, and Hondas. They pick vehicles that are reliable, practical, and hold their value.

That pattern still holds today. Recent surveys of affluent households show their average car is around 3 to 4 years old. Only about 25% of millionaires own a vehicle from the current model year.

Watches tell the same story. On the surface, it looks like wealth equals Rolex, Patek, or Breitling. In reality, most people with serious money don't use a $20,000 watch to tell the time. Daniel Craig has been seen wearing a Swatch. He can buy anything he wants. He just doesn't need a watch to show it.

Scroll through TikTok or YouTube and you will see luxury everywhere you look. It all looks like wealth, but most of it is financed or a paid advertisement. Those same videos never show the credit card statements or the stress when no one's looking.

The louder the performance, the thinner the margin usually is. The people financing Rolexes aren't the wealthy ones. They're the ones trying to buy credibility with a piece of jewelry.

This illusion isn't harmless. It drives people into debt by chasing an image. Luxury looks good online, but the question is whether it still feels good once the bill comes due.

That is what I set out to find out with my own survey.

Here's what the data actually shows.

SURVEY: DO LUXURY BUYERS REGRET IT?

I surveyed 200 adults who bought a luxury watch or handbag for at least $2,000 in the last five years. The survey was online and self-reported, with a margin of error of 7% at a 95% confidence level.

The results were clear.

85% said they didn't regret the purchase, and 80% said they would buy it again.

The people who were happiest shared the same habits. 59% checked every box. They paid cash, used the item as much or more than expected, had no regrets, and said they would buy it again. 78% bought it as a reward for themselves, not to impress anyone else.

The people who regretted the purchase broke that pattern in predictable ways.

13% regretted the purchase, and another 2% weren't sure. In the regret group, 36% bought because of image or social pressure. 27% barely used the item.

Age mattered too. Buyers ages 25 to 34 had the highest regret rate at 22%. It dropped to 11% for ages 35 to 44. No one over 55 reported regrets. Younger buyers were more likely to buy to look established. Older buyers waited until they were.

So how do you stay on the right side of that split?

Pay cash. If you need a card, it's not time yet. Buy it for yourself, not to prove something. Make sure you'll actually use it. If you can't name 5 times in the next 3 months when you'll use it, wait.

Don't even consider it until the rest of your plan is solid. Your emergency fund is full, retirement is on track, and the only debt you have is a mortgage.

Take a $3,000 watch. You have the cash saved on top of a full emergency fund. You've wanted the model for a year and plan to wear it every week. That matches the low-regret group. Buy it and enjoy it.

If you've already bought something and you're not thrilled, act fast. Return it if you still can. If it's sitting unused, sell it while it still holds value. Take the cash, fix the plan, and move on.

This survey measured how people felt after buying, not the quality of the product. The pattern was simple. People who bought with intentionality enjoyed it. People who bought to keep up didn't.

Most of what feels normal to you was modeled long before you earned your first paycheck.

YOU INHERITED A BROKEN PLAYBOOK

Imagine you inherited a playbook you never agreed to. The Joneses spend to look successful, and their kids pay the price for it.

From the street, it looks perfect. Inside, it's usually a mess of HELOCs, credit card balances, and Parent PLUS loans.

The numbers prove it. More than 3.6 million parents hold Parent PLUS loans, and the total balance has passed $110 billion. The average is about $30,000. That is more than a year of take-home pay for a lot of individuals.

I saw it back in college. Students talked about their loan balances, and some owed tens of thousands of dollars. Then I would see their Facebook photos. Their family looked rich online, but their kids were sinking in debt.

When that happens, options disappear. Kids start adulthood with loans instead of margin. Homeownership gets delayed. Job mistakes get more expensive. Parents want to help but can't, because there's nothing left to give. The spending looked fine in real time. The cost shows up years later, when flexibility matters most.

Kids grow up thinking that image is the goal and they repeat the same choices without even noticing.

Money habits are taught long before you ever touch a paycheck. Kids watch how their parents handle bills, debt, and savings. They learn if money is something to fear or something to use. Research out of Cambridge shows that money habits start forming by the age of 7. By adulthood, most people are running patterns they never chose.

Parents who overspend teach that debt is normal. Parents who save teach that discipline is normal. Parents who criticize every purchase teach fear. Those kids grow up second guessing every decision and avoiding real planning.

That script came from somewhere. It shaped how you think and how you react to money. You'll carry it unless you stop and name it.

Think back. Was debt normal in your house? Was spending celebrated? Was saving respected? Did anyone talk about money in a calm way? Your answers tell you what you were trained to repeat.

You have two paths. Keep copying the Joneses and end up in the same hole, or break the pattern and build something better. The Joneses aren't a model. They're a warning sign.

If what you learned doesn't build wealth, throw it out and write a new plan.

THE JANITOR WORTH $8M

Ronald Read spent his life doing work most people overlook. He pumped gas and worked as a janitor. He lived in a small house and drove an old Toyota. Nothing about him looked wealthy.

That's why his death in 2014 shocked his entire town in Vermont. Ronald Read was worth more than $8M.

He didn't win the lottery or build a company. He never earned a high salary. He lived below his means and invested for decades. He bought household-name stocks, reinvested dividends, and left it alone. Ordinary paychecks turned into real wealth because he gave them time.

When he passed away at 92, he left about $1.2M to his stepchildren and more than $6M went to his community. The Brooks Memorial Library called it the largest gift in its history. The local hospital called it transformative. The quiet man in flannel shirts left more behind than almost anyone in town.

Ronald's story exposes a hard truth. Plenty of people who earned far more have ended up with nothing. Celebrities and athletes burned through tens of millions. They had income, but no plan. Ronald had a plan. That's why his money lasted.

You don't need to copy his lifestyle to copy his results. His frugality was extreme, and it fit his personality. He could have afforded more but chose not to. That was his plan. Yours will look different.

You don't have to pinch pennies forever. You can take the trip or buy the car you planned for. The difference is that you do it with cash and a plan, not debt and stress.

Wealth doesn't have to be loud. It just has to last.

REMEMBER THIS

- Stop comparing. The highlight reel you see is not the full story.
- You don't have to be a star to build wealth.
- Lifestyle creep kills wealth at every income.
- Quiet money wins. Stop flexing and start stacking.
- Real wealth is invisible. It's the car not traded in and the payments you never took on.
- Luxury isn't the problem. Buying without a plan is.
- Anyone can build wealth with patience, consistency, and a plan.

CHAPTER 17

WHY YOU CAN, AND WILL BE A MILLIONAIRE

Most people look at the word *millionaire* and think it's a mountain too big to climb. The truth is that normal people hit it all the time. These are people who have never earned six figures in a single year but kept going. They didn't need luck. They had discipline and time.

If you invest $500 a month into an S&P 500 index fund, you hit $1M in 30 years with average returns. That's a car payment. Most people don't miss millionaire status because the math failed. They miss it because they never decided what saving would replace.

And that's only one account. Most households have several buckets growing at the same time. You hit seven figures long before any single account will.

THE NO-EXCUSE PLAN TO WEALTH

You built this in order. First came awareness, a starter emergency fund and stability. Then you burned the bridge to debt. After that you took control with a budget and sinking funds. Once the foundation was solid, you protected it with insurance and retirement accounts. Then you moved into wealth building by investing and not getting in your own way.

Here's the whole plan in one place.

THE NO EXCUSE PLAN TO WEALTH:

STEP 1: STOP THE BLEEDING

You start by taking inventory so you know where you stand. Then open a separate savings account and put something in it right away, even if it's only $50. From there, you build it up to $1,000 to $2,500 depending on your situation. You're done when that small cushion is in place. This keeps you from reaching for a credit card every time life throws you a bill.

STEP 2: KILL THE LEAKS

Next comes debt. Write down every balance you owe and decide the order in which you will attack them. Pay minimums on everything but the smallest and throw every extra dollar at that one until it's gone.

Then roll that payment into the next and keep going. You finish this step when every debt except your mortgage is wiped out. The payoff is simple. No payments mean your whole paycheck belongs to you.

STEP 3: LOCK THE SYSTEM

Build a budget that tells your dollars where to go. Add sinking funds so the big expenses are covered. You know you have reached the finish line for this step when every dollar has a job and you are no longer blindsided by car repairs, holidays, or insurance premiums. This is when guilt disappears and clarity takes over.

STEP 4: PROTECT AND PREPARE

Protect your progress. That means putting the right insurance in place so one accident or diagnosis cannot undo years of work. Fully fund accounts whose purpose is to secure your future.

Your HSA belongs here too. It shields you from medical surprises now and health costs later. You're done with this step when your money is safe and growing.

STEP 5: QUIET WEALTH

The last step is where your system starts working for you. You set up automatic investing in low-cost index funds and stay the course. The finish line isn't a single number but steady growth year after year as your net worth climbs.

The reason is simple. Compounding turns ordinary paychecks into extraordinary wealth.

THE VISION EXERCISE

Pick a date. At two years out, the debts are gone and the calls have stopped. Money is sitting in savings for the first time, and when the car breaks down, you just write a check and move on.

At 10 years, your net worth is rising fast. You're not guessing anymore. At 25 years, work is optional. The path to becoming a millionaire starts today with the step you choose next. You have the plan.

ORDINARY PEOPLE BECOME MILLIONAIRES

The majority of millionaires in America aren't celebrities, business moguls or athletes. They look like the people you see at work every day.

8 out of 10 millionaires are first-generation rich. That means they didn't inherit wealth. They didn't make superstar money. They made steady incomes and invested consistently. Most lived in normal houses, drove paid-for cars, and invested steadily.

They didn't chase flash. They were disciplined. And discipline beats income.

In 1935 Grace Groner bought $180 of Abbott Laboratories stock. She held it for decades, lived simply, worked as a secretary, reinvested her dividends, and by the time she died in 2010 her estate was worth more than $7 million. She never earned a high salary, but she let time and compounding do the work.

Anne Scheiber worked for the IRS. When she retired around age 51, she had about $5,000 in savings. She lived modestly, reinvested her earnings and allowed her money to grow over more than 50 years. When she died at age 101, her portfolio was worth about $22 million. Her late start didn't stop her.

BREAKING YOUR EXCUSES

What if you make little money? Then start small and cut harder. Even $50 or $100 a month compounds. Focus on increasing income over time with promotions, side hustles, or skill upgrades. Direction matters because consistency compounds. The starting point doesn't.

Starting late? Then you go aggressive. People in their 40s and 50s can still hit millionaire status if they cut expenses, kill debt, and invest aggressively. The window is smaller, but the math still works if you stay vigilant with savings and debt cuts.

Worried about crashes? They're normal. And markets have always come back stronger. The S&P 500 has returned an average of about 10% a year for nearly a century, through wars, recessions, pandemics, and political messes. If you stay the course, you win.

My survey of 400 homeowners showed that 56% of people end up prematurely dipping into their investments. Most fail because they interrupt their own plan. They never built enough margin to leave the money alone.

As an underwriter, I've seen what predictable patterns lead to the best outcomes. Money works the same way. When you follow the right steps, the results aren't a surprise. On this path, seven figures are the natural result of consistency over time.

AFTERWORD

I wrote this because I see the same patterns every day in my work. Companies get into trouble when they ignore risk or rely on luck instead of action.

Households fall into the same traps.

You can choose a different path. You've learned the steps and you now know how to use them.

I was the first test of this plan. I had to cut through advice that was loud, confusing, or flat-out wrong. I had to try things, fail, and adjust until a clear system formed.

What matters now is simple. You don't need a perfect start. You need follow-through. Outcomes change when behavior changes.

Money isn't the enemy. Unmanaged risk is. When you use money with intention, it stops being a source of stress and starts doing its job.

If you found this book helpful, I'd appreciate you taking a minute to leave a review wherever you bought it. Reviews help other readers discover the book.

REMEMBER THIS

- You control risk by controlling your choices.
- Income helps. Behavior decides.
- Simple steps, repeated, win every time.

No more pretending it'll fix itself. Be intentional.

—Josh Weaver

FREE RESOURCES

I've put the core worksheets from this system in one place.

It's called *The No Excuse Toolkit.*

These are the same tools I use myself. You can build your own if you want. This just saves time so you can focus on execution instead of setup.

THE TOOLKIT INCLUDES:

- **Debt Payoff Worksheet (Word)**
  See every balance in one place and track the exact order you're eliminating them.

- **Net Worth Tracker (Excel)**
  Track your real net worth so progress is measured, not assumed.

- **Budget Template (Excel)**
  Built around this book's system so every dollar is assigned before you spend it.

- **Emergency Fund Calculator (Excel)**
  Sets your emergency fund target based on your actual monthly spending.

- **Car Sinking Fund Calculator (Excel)**
  Plans your next vehicle now so you never need a car payment again.

- **House Down Payment Calculator (Excel)**
  Calculates your target and timeline so you know exactly what it will take.

The full kit is available here:

It's completely free. You don't need fancy tools to build wealth. You need consistency. These just remove friction.

ABOUT THE AUTHOR

Josh Weaver is a commercial underwriting consultant who reviews risk for a living. His job is to spot patterns early, understand how small decisions compound, and see where systems break before losses show up.

He brings that same lens to personal finance. After years of watching companies get into trouble by ignoring risk or relying on hope, he began applying the same principles to household money. The result is a practical system built around clarity, margin, and predictable outcomes.

Josh holds degrees in accounting and finance from Illinois State University. He's spent years testing these ideas in real life, adjusting what didn't work, and keeping what did. This book came out of that process.

He lives in Sarasota, Florida with his wife, son, dog, and cat. When he's not working, he's usually with his family, fishing, or learning about new tech.

BIBLIOGRAPHY

STEP 0: WHY YOU FEEL BEHIND WHEN YOU WORK HARD

- LendingClub. "Are Most Americans Living Paycheck to Paycheck?" 2024.
- Financial Planning Association. "The Propensity to Plan." *Journal of Financial Planning*, 2016.
- NerdWallet. "Compound Interest Calculator."

STEP 1: STOP THE BLEEDING

- Bankrate. "Most Americans Lack Savings for a $1,000 Emergency." 2023.

YOUR FIRST SAFETY NET

- CNBC. "Family Video to Close All Remaining Stores." 2021.

- Cleveland.com. "Why Family Video Outlasted Blockbuster." 2021.
- Federal Reserve. *Economic Well-Being of U.S. Households.* 2023.
- Federal Reserve. "Unexpected or Large Medical Expenses." 2023.

MAKING ENDS MEET (WHEN THEY DON'T)

- LendingTree. "Side Hustles and Financial Survival." 2025.
- Bankrate. "Side Hustle Participation Survey." 2025.
- Self Financial. "Side Hustle Dependence Statistics."
- Plan Sponsor Council of America. "401(k) Hardship Withdrawals and Loans." 2023.
- Side Hustle Nation. "Side Hustle Statistics." 2025.
- ZipRecruiter. "Food Delivery Driver Pay Data." 2025.

BURNING THE BRIDGE TO DEBT

- LendingTree. "Credit Card Debt Statistics." 2025.
- Debt.com. "Debt and Divorce Survey." 2023.
- *The Nilson Report.* "Credit Card Marketing Expenditures." 2024.
- *Journal of Consumer Research.* "Small Victories in Debt Repayment." 2016.
- Business Insider. "Best High-Yield Savings Accounts." 2025.

- S&P Global Mobility. "Average Age of Vehicles in the U.S." 2024.

SPEND WITHOUT GUILT

- Consumer Financial Protection Bureau. *A Closer Look at Emergency Expenses.* 2017.
- Gallup. "One in Three Americans Prepare a Detailed Household Budget." 2013.
- American Psychological Association. *Stress in America: Money.* 2022.
- Goldman Sachs Asset Management. Retirement Survey & Insights Report 2025: New Economics of Retirement. 2025.
- University of Kansas. "Pooling Finances and Marriage Quality." 2023.

THE NON-NEGOTIABLES

- Bankrate. *Emergency Savings Report.*
- Community State Bank of Colorado. "Recovering from Holiday Debt." 2025.
- Payless Power. "Using Sinking Funds to Pay Bills." 2024.
- CreditCards.com. "Holiday Credit Card Max-Out Rates." 2024.
- State Farm. "Budgeting for Home Maintenance."
- Williams, T. "Home Maintenance Costs Over $10,000." *Forbes*, 2024.

- MetLife Pet Insurance. "Emergency Vet Visit Costs." 2025.
- Bankrate. "Emergency Savings Withdrawals Hit Record Levels." 2025.

INTENTIONAL, NOT RESTRICTIVE

- LendingTree. "Credit Card Debt Statistics." 2025.
- SmartAsset. "Best Things to Buy Used." 2025.
- RefurbMe. "What Refurbished Really Means." 2025.
- Bankrate. "Americans' Biggest Financial Regrets." 2025.
- Gurliacci, D. "Household Waste in Clothing and Food." 2018.
- WRAP. "Unworn Clothing in Household Wardrobes." 2022.
- Royal Australian College of General Practitioners. "Clutter and Mental Health." 2019.
- WebMD. "How Clutter Affects Health." 2025.
- Fuller, K. "Clutter and Mental Health." *Verywell Mind*, 2023.
- Beckwith, A., Parkhurst, E. "Mental Benefits of Decluttering." 2022.
- Movinga. "Unused Clothing Statistics." 2023.

BREAKING THE CAR PAYMENT CURSE

- LendingTree. "Auto Loan Debt Statistics." 2025.
- Cox Automotive. "Average New Vehicle Transaction Prices." 2025.

- LendingTree. "Average Car Payment Statistics." 2025.
- NerdWallet. "Average New Car Prices." 2025.
- DemandSage. "Average U.S. Salary Statistics." 2025.
- Kelley Blue Book. "Vehicle Depreciation Rates." 2025.
- Kelley Blue Book. "Best Resale Value Awards." 2025.
- iSeeCars. "Infiniti QX80 Depreciation." 2025.
- AAA. "True Cost of New Car Ownership." 2024.
- Experian. "State of the Automotive Finance Market." 2025.

HOW TO BUY THE HOUSE AND KEEP YOUR LIFE

- Bankrate. "Mortgage Amortization Calculator."
- Redfin. "Average Homeowner Tenure." 2024.
- Weaver, J. *National Homeowner Survey.* 2025.
- Redfin. "Typical Homeowner Tenure by Region." 2025.
- The Zebra. "Average Length of Homeownership." 2024.
- Social Security Administration. "Normal Retirement Age."
- Gallup. "Retirement in America." 2024.
- Transamerica Center for Retirement Studies. "Employer Retirement Outlook." 2024.

WE ASKED 400 HOMEOWNERS. HERE'S WHAT THEY REALLY DID

- Weaver, J. *Mortgage Payoff vs. Invest Survey.* 2025.
- Federal Reserve Bank of St. Louis. "Why U.S. Home Prices Stayed Resilient." 2025.

- Federal Reserve Bank of San Francisco. "Pandemic-Era Housing Demand." 2025.
- Albanesi, S., De Giorgi, G., Nosal, J. "Housing Inflation and the Inflation Surge." NBER, 2022.
- Brookings Institution. "How CPI Accounts for Housing Costs." 2023.
- MeridianLink, Inc. Homeowner Equity Survey. 2025.
- Madison Trust. "Historical U.S. Home Prices." 2023.

DIAPERS AND DEGREES

- Redfin. "Family Help with Housing Costs." 2024.
- Care.com. "Cost of Child Care." 2025.
- Pew Research Center. "The Gender Pay Gap." 2023.
- Internal Revenue Service. "Child and Dependent Care Credit."
- Securities and Exchange Commission. "529 Plans Overview."
- U.S. Congress. *SECURE Act 2.0.* 2022.
- FSAFEDS. "Dependent Care FSA."
- Discover Financial Services. "Parents' College Cost Anxiety." 2023.

THE SAFETY NET NO ONE TALKS ABOUT

- Administration for Community Living. "How Much Long-Term Care You May Need."

- Social Security Administration. "Disability Benefits Statistics."
- Insurance Research Council. "Uninsured Motorists." 2023.
- National Association of Insurance Commissioners. "Auto Insurance Basics."
- Centers for Medicare & Medicaid Services. "EMTALA Overview."
- Consumer Financial Protection Bureau. "Medical Debt Burden."
- Internal Revenue Service. "Health Savings Accounts." Publication 969.
- Insurance Information Institute. "Life Insurance Basics."
- National Association of Insurance Commissioners. "Homeowners Insurance Shopping Guide."
- Insurance Information Institute. "Homeowners Insurance Basics."
- Harvard Joint Center for Housing Studies. "Renters Insurance Coverage Gaps."
- Genworth Financial. "Cost of Care Survey."
- Federal Trade Commission. "Identity Theft Reports."
- Centers for Disease Control and Prevention. "Travel Insurance Risks."
- U.S. Department of State. "Medical Emergencies Abroad."

HSA: THE MOST OVERLOOKED WEALTH TOOL IN AMERICA

- Devenir Research. *HSA Research Report.* 2024.

- Internal Revenue Service. "HSA Contribution Limits." 2026.
- Fidelity. "HSA Contribution Limits."
- Fidelity. "Planning for Health Care Costs in Retirement."

RETIREMENT: HOW TO WIN THE LONG GAME

- Bankrate. "Americans Behind on Retirement Savings." 2023.
- Vanguard. *How America Saves.* 2024.
- Internal Revenue Service. "Retirement Contribution Limits."
- Internal Revenue Service. "Required Minimum Distributions."
- Internal Revenue Service. "Early Distribution Penalties."
- Internal Revenue Service. "Backdoor Roth IRA Rules."
- Internal Revenue Service. "IRA Aggregation Rules."
- Internal Revenue Service. "403(b) Contribution Limits."
- Internal Revenue Service. "457(b) Contribution Limits."
- Securities and Exchange Commission. "Variable Annuities."
- Internal Revenue Service. "Solo 401(k) Plans."
- Internal Revenue Service. "Form 5500-EZ."
- Internal Revenue Service. "SEP Plans."
- Internal Revenue Service. "SIMPLE IRAs."
- Fidelity. "Retirement Savings Checkpoints."
- Social Security Administration. "Retirement Calculator."
- Bureau of Labor Statistics. "Retirement Spending Data."

- Administration for Community Living. "Long-Term Care Statistics."
- Internal Revenue Service. "IRA Contribution Limits."
- Fidelity. "Retirement Income Planning."
- Internal Revenue Service. "Retirement Plan Cost-of-Living Adjustments." 2026.

INVESTING: START SMALL, GROW BIG

- Damodaran, A. "Historical Market Returns." NYU Stern.
- Morningstar. "Bear Market History."
- Hartford Funds. "10 Things You Should Know About Bear Markets."
- S&P Dow Jones Indices. "Case-Shiller Home Price Index."
- DALBAR. *Quantitative Analysis of Investor Behavior.*
- Bogle, J. C. *Common Sense on Mutual Funds.*
- Vanguard. "Vanguard 500 Index Fund."
- Fidelity. "Fidelity 500 Index Fund."
- American Funds. "Washington Mutual Investors Fund."
- Nareit. "REIT Performance Data."
- Federal Reserve Bank of St. Louis. "Treasury Yield History."
- World Gold Council. "Gold Price History."
- S&P Dow Jones Indices. "S&P 500 Index."
- MSCI. "World and Emerging Markets Index Returns."
- Bureau of Labor Statistics. "Consumer Price Index History."

STOP COUNTING OTHER PEOPLE'S MONEY

- TheGrio. "Junior Bridgeman Obituary." 2025.
- Forbes. "Junior Bridgeman Net Worth."
- Weaver, J. *Luxury Purchase Habits Survey.* 2025.
- Spotrac. "Shaquille O'Neal Salary History."
- Celebrity Net Worth. "Shaquille O'Neal Net Worth."
- CNBC Make It. "Shaq's Best Financial Advice." 2021.
- Stanley, T. J., Danko, W. D. *The Millionaire Next Door.*
- *The Wall Street Journal.* "Millionaires' Car Preferences."
- White Coat Investor. "Drive a Beater, Get Rich."
- *South China Morning Post.* "Why Billionaires Wear Cheap Watches."
- Corder, R. "Daniel Craig and the MoonSwatch." 2023.
- NerdWallet. "Parent PLUS Loan Debt."
- Whitebread, D., Bingham, S. *Money Habits in Children.*
- Rick, S., et al. "Children's Money Attitudes."
- Hevesi, D. "Ronald Read Profile." *New York Times*, 2015.
- BBC News. "Ronald Read Fortune Story."
- Clifford, C. "How a Janitor Built an $8 Million Fortune." 2019.

WHY YOU CAN, AND WILL BE A MILLIONAIRE

- *Chicago Tribune.* "Grace Groner Estate Gift." 2010.
- *The New York Times.* "Anne Scheiber Obituary." 1995.
- Ramsey Solutions. *National Study of Millionaires.* 2019.

- Fidelity. "401(k) Millionaires Report." 2023.
- Federal Reserve Board. *Survey of Consumer Finances.* 2022.
- Spectrem Group. "Millionaire Households Report." 2023.
- Investopedia. "Long-Term S&P 500 Returns."
- Vanguard. "Retirement Income Calculator."
- Weaver, J. *Mortgage Payoff vs. Invest Survey.* 2025.